ISLAM AT THE

Also from Sophia Institute Press by Diane Moczar:

Ten Dates Every Catholic Should Know

DIANE MOCZAR

Islam at the Gates

How Christendom
Defeated the Ottoman Turks

SOPHIA INSTITUTE PRESS®
Manchester, New Hampshire

Sophia Institute Press®
Box 5284, Manchester, NH 03108
1-800-888-9344
www.sophiainstitute.com

Library of Congress Cataloging-in-Publication Data
Moczar, Diane.
    Islam at the gates : how Christendom defeated the Ottoman
Turks / Diane Moczar.
        p. cm.
    ISBN 978-1-933184-25-8 (pbk : alk. paper)
    1. Europe–History, Military–1492-1648. 2. Turkey–History–
Ottoman Empire, 1288-1918. 3. Europe–Foreign relations–
Turkey. 4. Turkey–Foreign relations–Europe. 5. Europe–Civiliza-
tion–Turkish influences. 6. Turkey–Civilization. I. Title.

D214.M63 2008

956'.015 — dc22

                                                          2007048862

Dedication

To Brother Bruno Bonnet-Eymard,
whose pioneering critical edition of the Qur'an
and original essays on Muslim religion and history
first aroused my interest in Islam.

Contents

Prologue. Muslim Aggression: A Drama in Five Acts . . . 3

1. The Ottomans Come on the Scene 23

2. Ottoman Success in the Fifteenth Century 43

3. The City Falls and the Heroes Die 63

4. The Suffering of the Balkans 83

5. Albania, Rhodes, Otranto 107

6. A Semi-Peaceful Interlude 123

7. Jihad at Sea 135

8. Hungary's Passion 159

9. The Anti-Jihad Victorious: Lepanto to Vienna
   and After 185

10. Islam at the Gates Once More 215

Select Bibliography 227

Index 237

Biographical Note 245

ISLAM AT THE GATES

Prologue

Muslim Aggression:
A Drama in Five Acts

On the Greek island of Santorini, monks secretly teach children religion and the Greek language — in defiance of their Turkish overlords. In the Balkans, parents desperately seek places to hide their little boys from Turkish kidnappers, who are coming with orders to fill their quota of captive children to send back to the sultan. On the Mediterranean, outnumbered Christian ships sail east to confront the Ottoman fleet in one of the great sea battles of history, while Christian princes struggle to put together a coalition army to take on the Turkish land forces. The popes repeatedly appeal for a new crusade, often in vain, and religious who have dedicated themselves to ransoming Muslim captives — even if at the cost of their own freedom — seek to save at least some of the multitude being taken for Turkish harems and slave labor. And the sultan's trusted general, an Albanian captive taken to the Ottoman court as a boy, abruptly changes sides during a crucial campaign and becomes the legendary leader of his people against the conquerors.

These are a few of the facets of what might be called "the anti-Jihad": the Christian resistance at all levels — from popes and priests, peasants and nobles, farmers and soldiers — in the face of the occupation of much of Christendom by Ottoman

Turks from the fourteenth to the early twentieth century. The resistance was not universal; some Christians collaborated with the invaders. Neither was it perfectly executed; politics often interfered with the West's military response, and what might have taken only decades with a wholehearted effort took centuries instead. Still, it was successful. The huge Ottoman Empire, one of the most extensive the world had ever seen, was reduced to the area of present-day Turkey. This is the story of the most glorious period of that resistance: that of the fourteenth century through the seventeenth.

The conflict between Islam and the West that has been in progress for the last eleven hundred years and is still ongoing can be viewed as a drama — a tragedy — in five acts; each act includes several scenes performed by many players. In this perspective, we are living in Act Five. The subject of this book is Act Four. Obviously, entering a theater near the end of a play leaves the playgoer at a loss, since he does not know what went on in earlier acts. We will therefore have to spend a little time reviewing the first three acts of our drama before bringing up the curtain on the fourth. Without some knowledge of the mentality, attitudes, and behavior of the early Muslims, we will not understand the motivation and behavior of the Ottoman Turks when we get to them.

Act One: The Emergence of Islam

In the mid-seventh century, Arab converts to a new religion began leaving Arabia for neighboring territories, taking their new faith with them. Over the next two centuries they spread north, east, and west and much of what was then Christendom fell to them, including North Africa, Spain, Palestine, and Syria.

Seventh-century Arabia would seem at first sight to be an unlikely place to spawn one of the great world religions. The northern part of the peninsula had been sporadically under Roman control and still maintained contact with Byzantium and other states. The southern tip of the peninsula had been influenced, and perhaps controlled, by the ancient African civilization centered in Ethiopia. The Queen of Sheba (or Saba) may have come from an ancient city in what is now Yemen. On the other hand, much of the interior of the land was populated by various tribes, some of them Jewish and many of them Christian, though their Christianity was often an unorthodox variety associated with various sects. There was also a large number of nomads who were polytheists.

A New Chosen People

When a new religion burst upon the scene, emerging full-blown in the text of one book — the Qur'an — it produced a great impact among a people who had previously been illiterate. Although the Qur'an is a large book with numerous sections (the *Suras*), some of them narrative and many dealing with minute regulation of the individual and social lives of believers, the essence of the new religion is simple. It posits one God, Allah, the existence of angels and of prophets (Jesus being one of the latter), and heaven and hell. It mandates five simple practices (the "pillars"), which include the ritual profession of faith that "there is no god but Allah and Muhammad is his prophet," prayer five times a day, fasting during the month of Ramadan, almsgiving, and a pilgrimage to the city of Mecca once in a lifetime. Many other regulations are also included in the Qur'an, such as circumcision and (possibly aimed at the Catholic sacrament of the Holy Eucharist) abstinence from alcohol.

The Qur'an cites the Bible in many places, but distorts the biblical passages it quotes in order to convey a new message. Its author seems to presume, for example, that justification originally came through circumcision, and that since Abraham's son by Hagar, Ishmael, was circumcised first, it was with him (traditionally considered the ancestor of the Arabs) that God made His covenant rather than with Isaac. Based on this example and others, some experts — including Brother Bruno Bonnet-Eymard, the French specialist in Qur'anic studies — have argued that the Qur'an's author intended neither to modify Judaism or Christianity, nor to create a third religion totally different from them, but rather to abolish them, in a *return* to what he sees as the original covenant of God with Abraham and Ishmael. (It goes without saying that the Jesus who appears in the Qur'an is not divine.) Thus, for Muslims, the Arabs are truly the chosen people, descended from Abraham's chosen son, called to restore the Temple and conquer the world for the God of the original revelation.

Results of the First Preaching of Islam

What followed the early promulgation of this new doctrine is somewhat obscure. Within Arabia, the new religious ideas brought strife to the whole peninsula. The polytheists fought the new followers of the one God, Allah; the Jews resisted being ruled by the new sectarians and many were massacred. Many — perhaps most — of the Christians seems to have managed to coexist and maintain amicable relations with the Muslims as long as the new religion was confined to the Arabian Peninsula. Possibly a sizeable number were attracted to the new faith and converted, though I have seen no reliable estimates of numbers.

As for what became of the creator of the new religion, Brother Bruno theorizes, from indications in the Qur'an and other sources, that he mobilized an Arab force that joined in the Persian and Jewish attack on Jerusalem in 614, which temporarily took the city from the Byzantine Empire. This enterprise apparently turned sour and the Arabs withdrew. When he died, in circumstances that remain obscure, his followers took his message and set off to spread it far and wide, by the sword when necessary.

This spreading of the religion of Allah, or at least Muslim rule, by the sword is usually referred to as *jihad*. The word refers to the obligation imposed upon all Muslims to engage in both a personal struggle for spiritual progress and warfare against non-Muslims. We will examine the concept in more detail below, since it was a major driving force in Turkish aggression against Christendom. It may be stated here that although modern Muslims often emphasize the spiritual meaning of the word, the emphasis in sources from the pre-modern Islamic period is on the military struggle to restore the whole world to the original religion of Allah and Islam.

The period of the emergence of Islam is particularly difficult for the historian to understand because of the lack of reliable sources. Except for the Qur'an itself, all the documents that Muslims use as sources for the life of Muhammad, which they claim embody authentic eyewitness accounts, date from fifty to a hundred and fifty years after the conventional date for the Prophet's death. Much of the material includes fantastic details that do nothing for its credibility and cannot be historically verified. Thus we are effectively left with one book, the little it tells us about "The Messenger" or "The Beloved" (the usual appellation for him, Muhammad, is a word that may, in the

Qur'an, be rather a description than a proper name), and more importantly, about his new religion. On the other hand, numerous contemporary sources record the impact of Arab raids on the populations that were eventually subjected to Muslim rule.

Following the later expansion of Arabian rule into neighboring territories, it soon became clear that both Christians and Jews would only be tolerated as second-class citizens, subject to onerous taxation and other humiliations unless they became Muslim. It is interesting to note that many Middle Eastern writers, including St. John Damascene, who worked at the court of the Caliph of Damascus in the early eighth century, considered the faith of the Arab raiders to be a Christian heresy, not a new religion. So many heresies had, after all, emerged within the sprawling Byzantine Empire that it was not easy even for contemporaries to sort them all out.

Religious Disarray in Byzantium

In fact, it could be said that the Greek part of the Roman Empire had always *been* prolific in spawning sects. In the early centuries of Byzantium, for example, there arose the significant heresy of the Monophysites, who held that there was only one nature in Christ, the divine. They were rivals of the Nestorians, who claimed (correctly) that there were two natures in Christ, but added (erroneously) that there were also two persons. Even though the Nestorians were condemned by the Council of Ephesus of 431, and the Monophysites at Chalcedon in 451, the ideas of both groups continued to circulate. Then there were the Monothelites, who countered that Christ has only one (divine) will, although they admitted the two natures and one person; thus, according to them, as man he had no will. They were supported by the early seventh-century Eastern emperor Heraclius, in the illusion that he might thus reconcile the warring religious factions that were not only jeopardizing spiritual unity but national security, since some of them seemed tempted to enlist the enemies of the empire in their cause.

The role that the emperors played in these religious quarrels had grave consequences for the future of the empire and all of Eastern Christianity, because their interference often caused tension between them and the popes in Rome. The Eastern emperors saw themselves as the watchdogs of Christian orthodoxy, and many of them came to resent any exercise of papal authority within their territory. Some were not above doing violence to papal emissaries and even to the person of the pope. Certainly the rulers of Byzantium had much to answer for in their frequent and sometimes brutal rejection of Catholic unity, even in these early centuries.

This confusing proliferation of sects worked in favor of the triumph of Islam in two ways. In the first place, the fact that Arab religious ideas could be seen as merely the views of a Christian sub-sect delayed realization of Islam's real menace as a new religion aimed at supplanting Christianity. Secondly, the existence of so many Christian sects prevented a unified resistance to the onslaughts of the new religion; each sect was so immersed in quarrels with the other sects and with Church authorities in Constantinople (who would themselves progress to rupture with Rome) that they all tended to ignore the truly serious danger until it was far too late. In many instances, short-sighted heretics actually attempted to enlist Muslim support in their religious quarrels.

Act Two: The Conquests

The beginnings of the great Arab conquest of neighboring lands are not well documented. Late in the seventh century there was undoubtedly fighting between Muslim and Jewish tribes within Arabia, and Arab raids on Byzantine territory soon afterwards, but it seems to have taken two centuries or more for significant parts of the Middle East to fall under Muslim rule.

The Arab conquest has been viewed so variously by historians that reading different authors can give the impression that they are describing events on different planets. Some historians paint stirring word pictures of massive Arab armies dashing out of the desert on their swift Arabian horses, killing, destroying, terrorizing, enslaving, carrying all before them and creating a new world based on Islam. Others question all the elements of the first view, some going so far as to characterize the conquests as "invisible." These writers assert that archaeological evidence does not support ancient reports of large-scale battles, widespread destruction of churches, and other devastation. They go on to say that the Arabs merely took over Byzantine and Persian administrative apparatus, which they left essentially unchanged, were very tolerant of non-Muslims, and were welcomed by many Christians and Jews as liberators.

Which is it? Fortunately this is a book about the Ottoman Turks so I do not have to give a definitive answer to this question. It appears, however, from a number of recent works, that the Arabs indeed brought misery, destruction, mass slavery and other evils to the areas they took over. They were "visible" all right. Surely the numerous eyewitness chronicles, treaties, and sermons by both Muslims and non-Muslims cannot be dismissed as so many forgeries for lack of archaeological support. (Partisans of the grimmer view, for that matter, also cite archaeological findings.) Everyone agrees that Arab rulers took over the administrations of the lands they conquered, but we also know that as soon as they could, they added their own stamp: for instance, there are surviving Byzantine gold coins that have had Qur'anic verses added to them.

The infiltration of Muslim Arabian tribes into neighboring territories was a process that could take many decades, depending on the area. Their task was facilitated in areas where there were already Arabs settled: in Syria, Egypt, Mesopotamia, and other Middle Eastern regions, they had only to be converted to Islam in order to be turned into allies of the occupation. Other Arabs, nomadic herdsmen, were part-time residents of the same areas and therefore seasonally available to fight the indigenous population.

The first raids — or *razzias* — were predatory attacks with which the lands bordering Arabia were all too familiar. What was new about them in the seventh and eighth centuries was that they were, increasingly, no longer brief incursions designed to scoop up booty and return to Arabia, but more organized attacks by men with a religious mission. When the raiders were reinforced by the resident Arabs and the nomads, their disorganized targets easily fell before them. Once this had happened, a new feature of the Arab presence developed: a rudimentary governmental organization designed to control the occupied territories and subjugate the population. Other Arabs were encouraged to migrate into the defeated territories, and these Arabs were not going home any more.

By A.D. 750 they had taken much of Mesopotamia and Armenia, the coastal areas from Syria to Egypt, and from there,

Christian North Africa. Then they crossed into Spain. Muslim armies continued to push north in exploratory raids into Europe until they were stopped by the Frankish leader Charles Martel at the Battle of Tours/Poitiers in 732. For centuries afterwards, Arab raiders and their Berber allies continued to harass the European coasts, for they had mastered shipbuilding with the help of conquered craftsmen, occupying Sicily for a time and even threatening Rome. Their final expulsion from Spain by the Spanish *Reconquista* in 1492 freed most of Western Europe from Muslim occupation, though by then the formidable power of the Ottoman Turks had spread into Eastern Europe and across North Africa, replacing Arab and Berber rule.

Muslim Culture

In the process of taking over everything in sight, the Arabs naturally appropriated the libraries (the ones they did not destroy) and learning of the Eastern Empire, which had survived the fall of Rome, and took notice of the architecture of the land they were taking over — so different from tents — even as they were torching Romanesque churches or turning them into mosques. Only dunces could fail to be impressed by the great civilization embodied in the books and buildings of the fallen, and the Arabs were no dunces, just sticky fingered. Among the literary treasures thus acquired were numerous classical Greek texts that were largely unknown in Western Europe, particularly major philosophical and scientific works. Arab scholars soon began to analyze and study this precious body of knowledge. Classical literature and history they largely ignored as being irrelevant or contrary to the principles of Islam. What remained of classical writings — including the voluminous works of Aristotle — they studied and annotated over the centuries. In this they were ahead of their fellow scholars in the north of Europe, who lacked both those works and competence in Greek. It is not that the scholars of Late Antiquity and the Carolingian period had no books. They had libraries full of numerous precious manuscripts, including a good deal of Roman literature, laboriously copied by hand over the centuries in the monasteries, and they also composed original works. There was, however, much that had been lost with the fall of Rome, particularly Greek philosophic texts.

This is where the Muslim centers of learning in southern Spain came in, as the texts they were studying and the translations that had been made — first by Syrian Christians into Arabic, and from that, again mostly by non-Muslims, into Latin — percolated north into Western Europe. The works of Aristotle in particular were to shape much of subsequent Western thought, beginning with St. Albert Magnus and St. Thomas Aquinas, though they had to be disentangled from the glosses added to the texts by Arab commentators before Aristotle could again speak for himself to the mind of the West. Thus the recently illiterate desert tribes developed a certain level of civilization and served as transmitters to the West of much valuable ancient learning.

As Arab rule spread gradually over the Middle East, Egypt, North Africa, and into Spain, its establishment was generally brutal, but that was true of all armed conflict of the period. What was distinctive about the new Arab regimes was their treatment of conquered peoples after they had submitted or been subdued; this evolved over time as Muslim religious authorities considered the questions raised by the rule of so many infidels and devised regulations that they were eventually able to implement, as we'll see in the next section.

The Status of Christians under Muslim Rule

Muslims distinguished Christians, Jews, and Zoroastrians from pagans, whom they were encouraged by the Qur'an to kill. In that same chapter (Sura 9, the "crusading chapter") we read:

> Fight those who believe not in Allah, nor the Last Day, nor hold that forbidden which hath been forbidden by Allah and His Messenger, nor acknowledge the Religion of Truth, from among the People of the Book, until they pay the *Jizya* [poll-tax] with willing submission, and feel themselves subdued. [Sura 9, A, 4, v. 29]

A commentary in my English translation remarks that this refers to "those who did not accept Islam, but were willing to live under the protection of Islam and *were thus tacitly willing to submit to its ideals being enforced in the Muslim State.*" (My italics.)

From this passage, it seems that A) unbelievers are to be fought until they submit, and B) the result of this violence will be a Muslim state enforcing its ideals. Elsewhere the same Sura says,

> The Jews call 'Uzair (Ezra) a son of Allah, and the Christians call Christ the Son of Allah. That is a saying from their mouth; (in this) they but imitate what the Unbelievers of old used to say. Allah's curse be on them: how they are deluded away from the Truth! [Section 5, v. 30]

This is pretty straightforward language that makes the Muslim view of Christians and Jews very clear. A later verse (33) goes on to reassure the reader that Allah will cause "the Religion of Truth . . . to prevail over all religions."

The question now arises as to what actual effect this teaching had on the first Muslims. Certainly the repeated injunctions to fight unbelievers found fertile ground in the hearts of Bedouins who lived by raiding and fighting. The waging of jihad did not die out, however, when the Arabs settled down. Each succeeding wave of converts, from Seljuqs to Mongols to Ottomans, took up the same war cry. Far from being a temporary feature of their early fervor, jihad became institutionalized as a permanent goal for all Muslim states as well as individual Muslims.

In the Muslim perspective, it is perfectly logical that Allah's usurped lands should be recovered for his people from the infidels, however long that might take and whatever means need be employed. Islam divides the world into two parts: one is the *dar-al-Islam*, or the abode of Islam, of peace and Muslim law, and the other is the rest of the world: the *dar-al-harb*, the abode of war. The inhabitants of the latter bring jihad upon themselves by refusing to accept Islam.

Theoretically, unbelievers were first to be summoned to convert and only attacked if they refused. In practice, the summons seems to have usually amounted to mere formality; it may have operated within limited areas, possibly within Arabia, where large groups did accept conversion rather than the grim alternative. By the time the Ottoman Empire was on the move west, however, one hears little or nothing of summons to conversion.

How did they treat conquered Christians, then? Surviving texts point to a body of legislation giving the warriors of Allah a wide range of options. Depending on their age, sex, and circumstances, captives could be killed, enslaved, ransomed, or liberated. The Qur'an itself refers to an arrangement (once again in Sura 9) by which conquered Christians and Jews — known as *dhimmi* — would be subjected to a tax, so long as they recognized themselves as "subdued." What did that mean in practice? To answer this question provisions, regulations, and admonitions proliferated from the pens of legal and religious authorities.

In general, the answer was that they should be so humiliated that whoever saw them would know they were unbelievers. The details of this humiliation evolved over time and varied somewhat according to circumstances. Still, as Bat Ye'or remarks in her masterly study, *Juifs et Chrétiens sous l'Islam*, the condition of the *dhimmis* was in some ways lower than that of the masses of slaves who served every Muslim society. The slave was deprived of his liberty, but could often rise to relatively high and responsible positions and sometimes even freedom, particularly if he were Muslim. The *dhimmi* on the other hand remained in his "subdued" state until he converted or died.

Other elements of the Muslim treatment of subject peoples may thus be summarized:

Destruction of places of worship — Numerous churches and synagogues were reduced to ruins throughout North Africa and the Middle East, even the Church of the Resurrection in Jerusalem, and new construction was forbidden. Christians kept trying, though. Depending on the whim of the reigning caliph, churches rebuilt surreptitiously were either demolished again or left standing; this probably accounts for some contradictions in the archaeological record.

Forced conversion — Although it was theoretically not to be forced on the conquered, exceptions proliferated. Also, the extreme pressure exercised by the threat of death, enslavement, deportation, destruction of one's home, and payment of tribute for which some lacked the means could well be summed up in the word "forced." Furthermore, parents who were unable to come up with the tribute money could have their children seized or become slaves themselves; either prospect was probably enough in many cases to produce at least outward acceptance of Islam. There are records of Christians in eighth-century Armenia and Syria being herded into churches and burned to death because they would not apostatize; elsewhere they were tortured, which often resulted (surprise!) in "conversion." In Spain in later centuries, the story was the same: perhaps thousands of Spaniards who refused to apostatize were martyred, while the whole Jewish population of Granada — some three thousand — was massacred in 1066.

Slavery — Muslims were by no means the only people to have slaves during the Dark and Early Middle Ages, but they turned the institution into an extensive and organized labor system that endured into modern times; in parts of Africa and Asia it apparently still exists today. Men were taken for labor, the women for exploitation by individual soldiers or within a ruler's harem. The number of slaves taken and deported could depopulate whole settlements; sometimes the men were massacred while the women and children alone were taken. Many thousands — sometimes tens of thousands — are mentioned in contemporary accounts; though ancient statistics are often unreliable, the number was certainly high enough to impress contemporaries as extraordinary. Intermittently there also appeared a practice that would take on a somewhat different — and more systematized — form within the Ottoman Empire. This was the requirement mentioned in treaties of the period for the regular furnishing of a certain number of slaves, usually annually, by a conquered town or region. Later we shall encounter the Ottoman variation on this practice.

Degradation of the dhimmi — The "subdued state" of conquered peoples who refused conversion to Islam, referred to above, was a highly visible and minutely regulated one. It appears that the earliest regulations drawn up were the strictest, while those of later Muslim periods, including the Ottoman, tended to vary according to region and circumstances. In contrast to earlier examples of state restrictions of various religious groups, it was the *humiliation* of the *dhimmi*, seen as a religious duty of Muslims in the face of the infidel's refusal to convert, that was unique. He was only suffered to live by virtue of the protection graciously extended to him by his Muslim lords, protection that could be withdrawn at any time should he rebel against his subjection. Such treatment unfortunately caused many demoralized Christians and Jews to convert to Islam.

Examples of the conditions imposed on the *dhimmis* included dressing according to strict rules governing color, type of belt, turban, etc. Christians were to behave humbly at all times, were not to ring bells or rebuild destroyed churches or monasteries, and were to provide three days' food and lodging in a church for any Muslim; they were also to step aside in the street, with visible humility, to allow Muslims to pass. Until modern times, under the Ottomans, Christians were forbidden to ride horses or use saddles; even official Western visitors to Ottoman Greece wrote of enduring long, painful rides on saddle-less mules. *Dhimmis'* houses were to be smaller than Muslims', certain places were off limits for them to visit, and until the twentieth century, in parts of the Middle East forced labor was required of them.

In *Juifs et Chrétiens sous l'Islam*, Bat Ye'or offers one example of just how picky the humiliating regulations could get. The fourteenth-century Muslim was advised by one Egyptian preacher, "When a *dhimmi* sneezes, one must not say to him 'God bless you,' but 'may God lead you to the right path,' or 'may he better your condition.' " I imagine one was to offer these wishes in a lofty manner, to emphasize one's kindly condescension toward that congested infidel who was clearly sneezing up the wrong path.

We will encounter more examples of what dhimmitude could mean for conquered peoples when we get to the Ottomans.

Act Three: The Seljuq Turks and the Crusades

The Crusades of the West were, of course, largely focused on the liberation of the Holy Land from the Turkish conquerors who had replaced the Arabs there in the late eleventh century. Europe had been far too weak during its Dark Ages to attempt any resistance to the Arab conquest of the Holy Land, but after a few centuries Arab rule began to weaken. The original Arab empire proved too far-flung to be long maintained by the Bedouin tribes that had started it. The conquest of civilized Persia, in particular, which soon converted to Islam, as well as the conversion of Berbers and various Asian tribes diluted original Arab unity, and the sheer scope of the conquered territory and the military campaigns required to maintain it, necessarily led to division. It was then that a new group began to filter into Western Asia.

The Eastern Empire had long been familiar with ethnic Turks, well before the rise of Islam. Sometimes they served as mercenaries in Byzantine armies, and sometimes they showed up on the other side, as members of Arab forces. By the eleventh century, however, one of those tribes from the steppe lands of Asia — the Seljuqs — had set up a powerful state on the eastern fringes of Anatolia, the area of the Byzantine Empire that corresponded in general to the Asiatic part of modern Turkey. Their aggressive campaigns won them control of Persia, Egypt, Mesopotamia, and other formerly Arab lands in western Asia, including the Holy Land. The disastrous battle of Manzikert in 1071 left Byzantium practically defenseless, its army destroyed, its historic eastern provinces captured, its churches and lands pillaged.

The attacks of these new marauders led the much-harassed Byzantine emperors to plead for help from the West. Pope St. Gregory VII was anxious to respond with military assistance for the empire; in 1074 he was writing to Christian princes asking for help, and in early 1075 he sent out a letter to the Christians of Europe "who wished to defend the Christian Faith," describing the atrocities of the Turks and the sufferings of the faithful in the East, who were being slain "like cattle," and attempting to mobilize the will and resources of the West to help them. Unfortunately he was unable to arouse enough interest among the knights of Europe, though he himself was willing to lead the expedition.

It was just twenty years later in 1095 that Pope Urban IV, receiving another urgent plea from Byzantium for European military aid, met with more success than Gregory. Perhaps the threat of the Turks to Christendom had become better known and appreciated during those twenty years, arousing a just anger in Europeans' hearts. In any case, the result of this new papal appeal was the Crusades — a long series of expeditions from the West to relieve the Eastern Empire and deliver the Holy Land from the infidel. (I hope it is very clear by this time that all along the Muslims, whether Arabs, Berbers, or Turks, have been the aggressors — the villains of this play, if you like — while the Christian states have been the victims of these largely unprovoked attacks.) As it turned out, the Crusades failed in their twin goals of liberating the Holy Land and saving the Eastern Empire, and they petered out after the death of the greatest of crusaders, King St. Louis IX, on crusade in 1270. The fateful consequences of the disastrous fourth Crusade will become apparent later in our story.

This emphasis on dislodging the Turks from the Holy Land is sometimes seen as an implication that the Seljuqs were harder on pilgrims than the Arabs, and the numerous reports of atrocities committed by the Seljuqs on pilgrims may have also helped produce that impression. It is worth pausing to look at this idea because so many textbooks do indeed contrast Seljuq barbarism with the ostensible tolerance and benevolence of the Arabs toward pilgrims visiting the Holy Land. The Arabs are thus presented as the "good" Muslims while the Seljuqs are the nasty ones.

The fact seems to be that both groups of Muslims persecuted Christian pilgrims. There are, for example, contemporary accounts of a large, unarmed group of German pilgrims who went to the Holy Land in 1064 and were attacked so violently by the Arabs that only 2,000, out of the original group of 7,000, returned home. They had been such a peaceful group that even under attack many of them refused to take up arms in self-defense, considering it a violation of their pilgrim status; thus their massacre was an unambiguous atrocity. A historian who researched and wrote about this "great German pilgrimage," calls the fate of those poor pilgrims "the most flagrant example on record of the persecution of occidental Palestine pilgrims prior to the crusades." Whether Arab or Seljuq, the Muslim occupiers of the Holy Land were never the friendly folk portrayed in so many modern textbooks.

So the curtain falls on the first three acts of the epic conflict we are examining, which spanned a period of approximately six hundred years. Act Four, when the Ottoman Turks come on stage, also runs for six hundred years. They were waiting in the wings, a motley group of nomads, until circumstances, their devotion to Jihad, and their own genius brought them onto the stage.

Main Works Consulted

Bonnet-Eymard, Brother Bruno. *Le Coran.*

Bolton, Andrew G., M.D., editor. *The Legacy of Jihad.*

Lewis, Bernard. *The Arabs in History.*

Ye'or, Bat. *The Decline of Eastern Christianity* and *Juifs et Chrétiens sous l'Islam.*

One

The Ottomans Come on the Scene

Probably no one in the thirteenth-century Middle East would have predicted the spectacular career of the Ottoman Turks. When they first came to the notice of people living in the Byzantine, Persian, or Seljuq empires, it was as merely one of many groups loosely known as "Turks" who had filtered out of the steppe lands of Central Asia and into western Asia. Like many other tribes, they ended up accepting Islam, or at least a sort of frontier version of it: a simple creed that they could live with and that fostered friendly relations between them and their many Muslim neighbors. It would soon become part of their identity and national motivation.

Beginnings of the Ottoman Imperium

Under a leader called Osman, from whom the word Ottoman ultimately derives, this tribe of Turks carved out for themselves a small territory with fluid boundaries at a time when all three major powers in the region — the Byzantine, Persian, and Seljuq empires — were in decline. The thirteenth century had seen two great incursions into the Middle East: the Crusades from the West, and from the Far East, the Mongol invasion. The Mongols destroyed much of the power of Persia and the Seljuq Empire, while Byzantium suffered the capture of Constantinople by Western forces during the Fourth Crusade in 1204 and the carving up of Greece and other parts of the Byzantine Empire into Latin-ruled principalities.

The goal of the crusaders in 1204 had been to help a claimant to the Byzantine throne take power in return for major religious and political concessions that would have helped the West substantially in its ongoing war against the Seljuq Turks. As it turned out, the claimant reneged on his promises, triggering the sack of Constantinople, the excommunication of the sackers by the pope, and the temporary occupation of much of the former Eastern Empire by Western Europeans.

By the end of the thirteenth century, Greek rule had been restored in Constantinople but the empire was a shadow of its former self, forced to accept the existence of Latin mini-states in its former Western provinces and semi-independent Turkish emirates on its eastern frontiers. Sometimes the emperors even called upon newly arrived nomads who were seeking their fortunes to help in Byzantine military campaigns. Osman's little group was only one of these tribes — considered so unimportant, in fact, that little was written about it by contemporary chroniclers.

It is known that Osman defeated a Byzantine army in the battle of Baphaeon (or Bapheus) near Nicomedia in 1301, which enhanced his prestige among his people. For the Greeks, it was probably viewed as merely an unfortunate incident, but in fact it was to be succeeded within the next few decades by victory after victory for the tribe of Osman, now known as *Osman Bey* or General Osman. Under his son, Orhan Bey, the tribe began to expand further and attract recruits from other tribal conglomerations. Stupidly — as it appears in hindsight — it was the Byzantine government itself that gave them their first boost onto the stage of Western history, as we shall see.

The Role of Islam in Ottoman Life

Here we should pause briefly to consider the question of how much the rise of the Ottomans was motivated by their religion. Like many other Turkish tribes on the Byzantines, Osman's group had embraced Islam. Older Western historians of the Ottomans tended to ascribe to the warrior *ghazis* a particularly fervent dedication to Islam and its spread. (The very term, *ghazi*, used by the Turkish warriors for themselves as fighters for Islam seems to come from *gaza*, which means holy warfare — jihad, in fact, in Turkish.) Later historians took issue with this view and tended to downplay the role of religion in the Turkish conquests. These Turks, they argue, were simply motivated by the lure of booty and power, and happened to have leaders capable of winning their loyalty and planning victorious campaigns. Their history would have been essentially the same no matter what their religion or lack of it.

This may be a case of viewing the past through the distorting lens of modern secularism. Certainly some of the most recent scholarly writing on the topic seems to confirm the older view. Thus Bernard Lewis writes in *The Middle East*,

> The classical *jihad* against Christendom was resumed by the Ot-
> tomans — of all major Muslim dynasties, the most fervently and
> consistently committed to the Muslim faith and the upholding and
> enforcement of the Holy Law. In the early centuries of Ottoman
> history, *jihad* forms a major theme in their political, military, and
> intellectual life alike, and it is clear that the Ottoman sultans, at
> least until the time of Suleyman the Magnificent, were sustained
> by a high sense of moral and religious purpose.

Other scholars, relying on early Ottoman sources, have also remarked on the continuity between the jihadist mentality and

practices of the Ottomans and those of their Muslim Arab and
Seljuq predecessors. We will see evidence of this as we move
through the Ottoman adventure. It seems to me that if one takes
into account the unique role of the dervishes in Ottoman society,
discussed below, it is clear that far deeper considerations than
those of mere economic and political gain motivated Ottoman
expansion.

The Ottomans Enter Europe

It is strange how little significance contemporaries often see in
the most momentous events in history, though to later generations their importance becomes glaringly apparent.

The year 1354 marked a fateful moment in the history of
Europe, as well as in the histories of the Byzantine and Ottoman
Empires, yet only a few men living at the time seem to have
grasped it. Orhan Bey had gone from strength to strength in the
years preceding 1354, even receiving the daughter of a claimant
to the Byzantine throne for a wife, in return for his support of
her father. He had also consolidated control over much of the
former Byzantine territory in Asia Minor, through a number of
policies formerly utilized by Arab and Seljuq conquerors. Occupied territory was divided into districts populated by new Turkish landholders and other colonists, including soldiers, slaves,
and those taxpaying *dhimmi*. The landowners held the land
for the sultan, who was considered to own all of it. Although
many of the country people fled to the towns and cities as the
Turks advanced, there were always collaborators: disgruntled
Monophysites and members of other sects with a grudge against
the Orthodox Church, as well as those on the outs with the
Byzantine government often supported the Turks, and the Turks

were shrewd enough to keep their tax rates low enough — at least in the beginning of any occupation — to undercut what the local government had been collecting. Mosques were built and many Christian churches became mosques. The whole Muslim religious apparatus of clergy, preachers, teachers, and so on took root, and over an extended period the demographic balance, shifted in the Turks' favor. This whole process was already underway by Orhan's time — when the Ottomans had reached the shores of the Dardanelles and controlled the passage across the Dardanelle straits into Thrace — and he built upon it.

Europe must have appeared as an attractive new frontier for a powerful chief who thought big. It is true that some of the other Turkic tribes had earlier reached the Aegean and raided the Greek islands and even the Greek mainland, but they abandoned that policy upon encountering resistance by the Latin colonizers in the area and losing a seaport on the Turkish coast. An excursion into Europe in some other direction was clearly indicated, and it was the Byzantines themselves who provided the opportunity. John Cantacuzene was a usurper who had been regent for the legitimate heir, John V, but took power for himself, touching off a civil war. It was he who enlisted Orhan Bey's help several times, in campaigns against an upstart Serbian chief in Macedonia and a Bulgarian-Venetian force that was supporting another claimant to the throne, and other military endeavors. The Ottomans obligingly provided several thousand horsemen, and in the historic battle of Demotika in 1352 decisively defeated the Serb army. As John V. A. Fine, Jr. remarks in his *The Late Medieval Balkans*, "The battle near Demotika was the first major battle between Ottomans and Europeans in Europe and its results made Dušan [the Serb leader] realize that the Turks were a major threat to Eastern Europe."

The danger grew when Orhan's son, Suleyman Bey, to whom his father had entrusted the area bordering the Dardanelles, took a fateful step. Although the Turks had crossed to the European side more than once, they had always returned to Asia. In 1354, however, in the course of one of the many campaigns the Turks undertook in alliance with the Byzantine army, Suleyman Bey captured the castle of Gallipoli (easily, because it had just suffered an earthquake) and held onto it as a base for further expansion into Europe. From the peninsula of Gallipoli, the Ottomans, still directed by the formidable Orhan, could raid Byzantine territory on the other side of the Straits. This was Thrace, an agricultural area important to the empire both because of its food production and the taxes paid by its landowners.

In the years immediately prior to the Turkish takeover, Thrace had suffered Bulgarian raids, depopulation from the Black Death, and other turmoil. Thus one of Orhan's first moves was to bring over Ottoman settlers from the Asiatic side of the Hellespont to colonize the region. More Turkish chiefs followed with their military contingents, taking over the lands of fleeing Christians. For the first time, numerous Turkish immigrants had settled within Europe. From Thrace, they would gradually expand their holdings into Bulgaria and other Balkan areas. Just so had barbarian hordes filtered into the doomed Western Roman Empire in the fourth and fifth centuries; just so, also, had the Arabs expanded northward, once they had crossed from Africa into Spain. Unlike the Arabs, however, the Ottoman Turks would prove so tenacious that not even major setbacks and military defeats would stop their relentless progress ever further toward the heart of Europe.

Ottoman Methods of Conversion

In Thrace, the Turks employed methods for converting the Christian population already being practiced with some success in Anatolia. Here it seems that a crucial role was played by the dervishes: members of a sect of Islam that included many varieties of what is usually called mysticism, one branch of which is the famous whirling dervishes. (Not all dervishes whirled.)

Some groups of dervishes fought in the military, and we will see later what effect they had on the Western armies they encountered. The dervishes also promoted the development of the Ottoman Empire and the Islamization of conquered lands in several ways. In the first place, it seems to have been they who kept up the spirit of jihad among the ghazis, through their preaching and exhortations to holy war. Secondly, some of their leaders possessed such stature within the Ottoman state that their favor, or lack of it, was important in guaranteeing the authority of Turkish rulers. Furthermore, precisely because of their heterodoxy they were successful go-betweens for Muslims and Christians; they even seem to have professed some Christian religious ideas. Lastly, they were able to use these shared ideas — the veneration of some Christian holy places, for instance — to draw ill-instructed Christians into a gradual acceptance of Islam.

The process was not as successful in Europe as it had been in Anatolia, but it was devastating enough. Thus many Christians, those who remained alive after the Muslim attacks and had not been enslaved, were induced to convert to the religion of their conquerors. There were also, of course, the opportunists mentioned above who converted in order to curry favor with their overlords or to keep their lands, political positions, or

possibly their children. Especially in formerly Christian areas
such as Thrace, where sizeable numbers of Turkish colonists
had been brought in and numerous Christians had fled or been
enslaved, the remaining Christians were all too likely to end up
merging with the new arrivals and losing their faith.

The result was that many rural areas, which had been Christian for many centuries, became solidly Muslim. For the time
being, Byzantine citizens in towns and citadels were left unmolested, but everyone must have known that this was a temporary situation. The first steps toward Ottoman conquest of the
Balkans, Greece, Hungary, and what remained of the Byzantine
Empire, by both military force and immigration, had been taken.

The Byzantine Predicament

The Eastern Empire was increasingly squeezed into a desperate little enclave around Constantinople and a few other holdings from which the capital was largely cut off. The usurping
emperor was totally discredited, and his pleas for help from the
Balkan Christian powers met with no response except reproach.
He had brought about the disaster, they sneered, by his foolish
reliance on the Turks as allies. Let him take the consequences. An
uprising within Constantinople itself caused the acting emperor
to abdicate and retire to a monastery in Greece.

His legitimate replacement, John V Palaeologus, found himself
in an even more humiliating position than his predecessor. The
balance of power had been completely reversed: instead of the
Turks being vassals of the Byzantines, the Byzantines found themselves so weak that they had practically become Turkish vassals.
For example, John was ordered by the sultan to rescue the Turk's

nephew from pirates who had captured him. This resulted in the ridiculous situation of Turkish forces besieging Byzantine forces in Thrace while the Byzantine fleet was off attacking pirates at the Turkish leader's behest. The episode of the captive nephew dragged on for over a year. The Byzantine fleet failed to defeat the pirates and Sultan Orhan ordered the emperor to try again, which he humbly did. Finally, the fleet refused to continue the siege and the sultan changed his tune: now he demanded that the emperor cough up a huge ransom for the captive and also give his ten-year-old daughter to the sultan in marriage. These things were done, and the child was betrothed to the Turk in a Muslim ceremony.

John V did not abandon hope for the survival of his empire. For the first time, an emperor of Byzantium traveled to Europe to beg help for his besieged realm. In 1365–1366 he was at the court of King Lajos the Great of Hungary, pleading for aid. This monarch was known for his zeal in the struggle against the Turks, and was farsighted enough to maintain a number of *banats*, fortified frontier areas in the Balkans, to serve as buffers against invasion. In one papal letter he is called "Christ's shield; the Lord's athlete" because of his zeal for the conversions of pagans and heretics and his promotion of missionary activity in the Balkans. A peace-loving monarch, he was nonetheless repeatedly drawn into wars to defend the interests of the papacy or the security of his own realm.

Yet he apparently refused to help John V. The reasons are obscure. Some have assumed that the emperor's Orthodoxy was the obstacle, though there are numerous examples of other Orthodox Byzantine rulers receiving help from the West against Muslim aggression. Furthermore, John was probably already willing to convert to Catholicism and would no doubt have mentioned this to the king, in which case his religion would not have been a problem. Whatever the reason, the king of Hungary mysteriously refused any help.

The emperor then suffered the humiliation — by no means the last — of being refused permission by the Bulgarians to cross their territory on his way home. He was forced to remain in Hungary until his cousin, Count Amadeus VI of Savoy, came to his assistance with his army and forced the Bulgarians to let the emperor pass. John realized, of course, that the schism between the Orthodox and Catholic Churches and the extreme hostility felt by many Orthodox for Rome made it all the harder to elicit sympathy from Catholic Europe. Even Petrarch, the Italian Renaissance scholar, wrote that "the Turks are enemies, but the Greeks are schismatics and worse than enemies."

The Emperor and the Saint

When we follow John back to Constantinople, we unexpectedly meet a saint — and a saint in an unexpected role. St. Peter Thomas was a Carmelite with a reputation for holiness who had been serving as papal legate in the East since 1359, working for reconciliation of the Orthodox with Rome and the strengthening of alliances against the Turks. Assisted by the Venetians and the Knights Hospitaller, he also led a successful assault on a Turkish base on the Anatolian side of the Dardanelles. It was not of great significance, but Peter Edbury, in *The New Cambridge Medieval History*, notes that it was the first time since 1261 that a Western crusade had brought military assistance specifically to support a Byzantine emperor. Unfortunately, St. Peter was then dispatched to Cyprus and in 1366 he seems to have been leading an attack on the Muslims in Alexandria when, at the age of sixty-one, he was badly wounded and died three months later.

Opinion seems divided on whether that makes him a martyr, but anyway he is a saint and one whom the emperor must have sorely missed. In the following century we will meet another monk, also drawn from the cloister to join the grim struggle against the Turks; he also died following a great battle. The example of these two champions of God recalls their predecessor, the twelfth-century Cistercian St. Bernard of Clairvaux, who only wanted to live a cloistered life but was instead thrust into the turmoil of the crises of his time, tirelessly preaching crusades and writing a rule for an order of warrior monks. Monks in those days were not pacifists. It may well have been St. Peter — the heavenly original as well as the namesake — who determined John to make his submission to the Church. The year after his harrowing return from Hungary he was off to Europe again, this time to see Pope Urban. He would return a Catholic.

The Emperor in Rome

The popes had seen the danger posed by Muslim aggression for over three hundred years. Thus Pope Urban V tried to rally Christian resistance against Islam in the early 1360s by calling for support of the Byzantines — even without their conversion. In this he was following the example of his predecessor, Urban II, who had called the First Crusade at the request of the Eastern emperor; unlike the speech of Urban II at Clermont, however, the plea of Urban V fell on ears that were mostly deaf. It is true that there was still at this time some crusading fervor among the knights of Europe, and some expeditions were organized. Most were not directed at the Ottomans in Europe, however, but toward the Holy Land, not yet in Ottoman hands, or against the Mamluks of Egypt.

Urban V moved temporarily from Avignon to Rome in 1367. It was while he was in Rome that, in an extraordinary move, John V came to meet him and formally converted to Catholicism. During an impressive ceremony in St. Peter's he confirmed his profession of faith, including the points on which the Orthodox schism had occurred: the procession of the Holy Spirit from both the Father and the Son, and the universal authority of the pope. Pope Urban then wrote an encyclical expressing both his joy at the emperor's return to the Faith and his hope that it would become a precedent for other Orthodox. The Patriarch of Constantinople, on the other hand, sent messages all over the Orthodox world urging steadfastness in schismatic beliefs and practices. John's conversion thus remained a personal act, which failed to move his people and in fact aroused their opposition. A further humiliation awaited the emperor on his way home from Rome when he was detained in Venice as a debtor; his eldest son refused to pay his debt and it was a younger son, Manuel, who came to his father's aid.

Still the trials of this courageous and well-meaning (though tragically ineffective) man were not over. The obnoxious eldest son rebelled against him, in collusion with the Ottoman sultan Murad's son rebelling against *his* father, and was imprisoned. He was released with the sultan's help, and Murad demanded that all the guilty parties, including both his son and John's, should be punished. He summarily executed many of the Greek rebels, and had his own son blinded and then beheaded, ordering the fathers of the rebels' Turkish supporters to do the same; two who refused were themselves killed. Now Murad insisted that John blind his own rebellious son and the little grandson who had joined him. The job — usually performed with boiling vinegar

— was bungled somehow (no doubt due to John's kindness) and the sight of the guilty ones was only temporarily impaired. Even so, John felt obliged to send an apology to the pope for having agreed to the terrible deed; he received a kindly and understanding reply.

Incredibly, there is more to what we might almost call the martyrdom of this Catholic emperor — so vilified in contemporary Orthodox accounts of his life — but we cannot follow him through it all in detail. More rebellions, more betrayals, more crosses. He was forced at one point to lead Greek forces to support Turkish campaigns, and in 1390–1391 his faithful son Manuel, now his co-emperor, also had to fight with the Ottoman army in an expedition against both other Turkish emirates and Christians in Asia Minor. We have Manuel's record of the hardships of that campaign, and the intense suffering he endured at the sight of destroyed Christian cities. Above all, it was the thought that they were actually helping their archenemy that sickened him. In one of his letters he remarked bitterly, "but one thing is unbearable for us: we are fighting with them and for them [the Turks] and it means that we increase their strength and decrease ours."

Once more at home, John rebuilt some of the defenses of Constantinople — not yet under Turkish rule — but the sultan forced him to destroy them. Possibly he would have been glad to refuse one of these demands and die for it, had he not feared for the fate of his son and his people. He knew only too well what the Ottoman army was capable of doing to the defenseless peasants outside the walls of the capital, and to those towns and regions that still remained under Greek control. In 1391 he finally and mercifully died, and was succeeded by Manuel.

The Response of the West

It would not be true to say that the West completely ignored the plight of the Eastern Empire while all this was going on. In addition to the naval league mentioned above, an army of Serbs and Hungarians had marched on the Turks in 1363 and had been nearly annihilated. This aroused genuine alarm in some quarters, and a desire on the part of at least a few leaders to offer assistance against the Turks in response to the anguished pleas of John V. Charles IV, Holy Roman Emperor, seems to have visited Avignon and urged Pope Urban V to call a crusade against the Turks in 1363. This did not materialize, but the pope continually promised aid to Emperor John V, before and after his conversion, and urged King Lajos of Hungary and other Catholic leaders to military action.

Only one of them, John's cousin Count Amadeus VI of Savoy, seems to have taken the idea of a crusade, an anti-jihad, to heart. Amadeus actually set off with an army and managed to recapture Gallipoli, but by then the Turks were already in Europe in such large numbers that it hardly mattered. We have also seen above that Western forces continued to make sporadic attacks on Muslim strongholds during this time. The fact is, however, that most countries of Europe were suffering some sort of turmoil of their own. Some of it was due to the dislocations caused by the Black Death, some to the ongoing Hundred Years' War between England and France and to the proliferation of armed and warring factions in Spain, Italy, and elsewhere. As for the Balkans — the crucial target of the Ottomans' next campaign in Europe — they were hopelessly fragmented. The various areas of the peninsula populated by Serbs, Bulgarians, Croatians, Albanians, Venetians, and other groups were divided both ethnically and religiously, while the struggle of the stronger families to carve out viable states at the expense of their rivals was constant.

It would take ninety-nine years from the first capture of Gallipoli for the Turks to take Constantinople, but the Ottomans were in no hurry. They had already begun thinking of where else they might go. By the early 1360s Orhan was dead, and his younger son Murad had come to the throne. Kinross calls him "the first great sultan," and states that "Thanks initially to Murad, the West was now to fall to the East as the East had fallen to the West in the centuries of the Greeks and the Romans." It is to Murad also that some sources trace the emergence of the institution of *devşirme*, and since we will soon encounter it again — repeatedly — this may be the place to introduce it.

The Fate of Christian Children under the Turks

Devşirme was the "boy tribute" routinely collected by the Turks from conquered peoples. It took different forms as it developed, but everywhere it was practiced it meant that parents were forced to hand over some of their male children to the Turks. Possibly the precedent for this was the earlier Muslim practice of requiring certain conquered towns and regions to furnish a yearly quota of slaves. Ottoman conquerors took masses of slaves, men, women, and children, as we will observe, but the requisitioning of boys in particular was made a regular system subject to minute regulations. It is estimated that about a fifth of the children of Eastern and Central Europe were taken by the Turks as tribute; collection seems to have varied according to the needs of their Turkish overlords in the beginning, and later became an annual practice in some places.

Devşirme typically involved seizing boys aged fourteen to twenty and training them for diplomatic and military roles in the growing Ottoman Empire. Recruitment agents would choose the fittest and most attractive boys and take them away to the court of the sultan, where they were raised as Muslims (possibly forced to submit to an excruciating circumcision) and trained extensively for their new roles, including service in the Janissary corps, the elite Ottoman infantry composed almost entirely of former Christians. They would never be allowed to marry or own property, but they could rise to relatively high positions of authority.

A similar Ottoman institution was the *içoglan*, a variation of the *devşirme*, involved the collection of little boys six to ten years of age. They too were converted to Islam, shut up in the sultan's palace under the care of eunuchs, and rigorously trained for fourteen years, after which they filled positions in the sultan's administration.

Even within this cruel system there was room for corruption and the possibility of an even worse fate for the captives. The kidnappers might take more children than they needed and try to sell the rest back to the parents. If the parents could not pay the price — more anguish for them — the boys would become ordinary chattel slaves, with few prospects for advancement, or be sold in a slave market. To forestall escape, the boys could be transferred to distant areas and put under the harsh care of Muslim lords. Those who did succeed in running away and returning home would find their fathers cruelly punished, which discouraged further escape most effectively. Then there was the appalling anxiety of the parents, especially in view of the Turks' practice of taking boys who were attractive as well as robust, that they would end up as victims of Turkish pederasty. Although the practice is technically forbidden by the Muslim religion, there are many references to it in historical records, especially those left by Western travelers to the Middle East, stories that rumors among the conquered would have elaborated. Even if only some of such reports were true, it would be enough to sicken any parent watching his child depart with the Janissaries.

There is a tendency on the part of some admirers of the Ottomans to minimize these atrocities. More than one historian of the Ottomans has excused the two practices described above as the equivalent of sending a child away for a prestigious education and training for a lucrative career. They have described *devşirme* and its variations as a means of betterment for the rustics of Europe, who would have been much better off in the civilized and refined court of a sultan who paid them well. This view sounds incredible, even granting the possibility that the authors who espouse it have no little boys of their own. Surely, the agony of parents deprived of their sons and that of the boys snatched from their families and thrust into an alien world is nothing short of traumatic and tragic for all concerned. But what, ask the obtuse authors, would the boys really lose? In most cases, they assert, peasant status, hard labor in the fields, poverty; and in return, they get riches and glory. What more could they ask for?

Their mothers, perhaps; their families, their native land, their Faith — the greatest loss of all. Indeed, the extreme pressure to which they were subject, added to the isolation from all Christian contacts, would seem to have been the equivalent of the kind of brainwashing that would later produce converts to atheistic Communism.[1]

---

[1] "But didn't you forget to mention the consideration and thoughtfulness of the Turks in this business?" their stubborn admirers murmur. "Remember that only sons were not taken, nor were the sons of widows, for instance." Yes, that was big of them. I've mentioned it now.

In 1456, a pathetic appeal from Greek Christians living in Asia Minor, highlighting their concern for their children, was sent to the Knights of Rhodes:

> We . . . inform your lordship that we are heavily vexed by the Turk, and that they take away our children and make Muslims of them. . . . For this reason we beseech your lordship to take council that the most holy pope might send his ships to take us and our wives and children away from here, for we are suffering greatly from the Turk. [Do this] lest we lose our children, and let us come to your domains to live and die there as your subjects. But if you leave us here we shall lose our children and you shall answer to God for it.

Even if the Knights had tried to respond to this desperate plea — and we don't know if they did — the strength of the Ottomans in Asia Minor in 1456 would have been too much for them.

The large-scale bloodletting caused by taking so many boys from conquered Christian communities led to a decline in the Christian population to the benefit of the Muslims; it is estimated that between half a million and a million Christian boys, mostly from the Balkans, were victims of this brutal system from its inception until its abolition in 1848, and this does not include the numerous other slaves taken by the Turks.

Thus, with the accession of Sultan Murad, the makings of the Ottoman Empire were all in place: a foothold in Europe, a strong military with a steady supply of captive recruits, masses of slaves to attend to all the details of daily life, and a determination to spread Islam, as a later sultan would put it, "from east to west." Christendom little knew what peril it was to face in the next two centuries.

MAIN WORKS CONSULTED

Baynes, N. H., and Moss, H. St. L. B., editors. *Byzantium.*

The Cambridge Medieval History, vol. V, relevant articles.

Fine, John V. A., Jr. *The Late Medieval Balkans.*

Kinross, Lord. *The Ottoman Empire.*

Lewis, Bernard. *The Middle East.*

Pastor, Ludwig von. *History of the Popes*, vol. I.

Vardy, S. B., *et al.* editors. *Louis the Great, King of Hungary and Poland.*

Vasiliev, A. A. *History of the Byzantine Empire*, vol. II. The quotation from Manuel II is found on p. 587.

Vryonis, Speros, Jr. *The Decline of Medieval Hellenism.* The quotation from the letter to Rhodes is on p. 241.

Ye'or, Bat. *The Decline of Eastern Christianity.*

Two

Ottoman Success in the Fifteenth Century

It should not be forgotten, as we follow the Turkish armies now swarming through the Balkans, that their European conquests would come to represent only a part of the enormous empire they eventually ruled. When we look at a map of the Ottoman Empire at its height in 1683 — stretching from Tunisia to Arabia, through most of the Middle East to the Persian Gulf, encompassing the Balkans, Greece, nearly all the Mediterranean islands, Hungary, and Central Asian regions bordering Russia — it's hard to believe that Europeans could have failed to perceive their danger during its emergence.

In defense of our shortsighted ancestors, however, it is worth considering the view from Europe in the last decade of the fourteenth century. At that time, most of the regions that would end up on the Turkish imperial map remained to be conquered. There were still emirates in Anatolia ruled by other Turkish tribes that had not yet been gathered in by the Ottomans. Egypt, Mesopotamia, Arabia, North Africa, Hungary, Bosnia, Albania, Greece, and large portions of the Balkan Peninsula still remained beyond the sultans' grasp; some of those areas would not be acquired until the end of the seventeenth century. Without totally excusing the shortsighted, then, we can at least try to imagine how the Ottoman advance into southeastern Europe

would be mainly of concern to the people in its way, and those
— such as the Hungarians and some Italians — who recognized
the drawbacks of having the Turks as near neighbors. The rest
of Europe saw no immediate need to worry. Besides, didn't it
serve those obstinate Orthodox right, for the contempt they had
always shown for the Catholic religion and its head?

As had been the case so often in earlier Western history, it
was mainly the popes who took the long view. But although
they remained seriously alarmed as the year 1400 dawned, their
own problems may have seemed more urgent than the Turkish
menace. The Great Schism of the West, for example, had divided
Christendom since 1378 on the question of who the true pope
actually was. The decades of rivalry between two and sometimes
three claimants to the papal throne would only end in 1417;
thus, during a crucial period in the development of the Ottoman
Empire, papal authority was seriously compromised.

The Conquests of Murad and Bayazid

The records of Murad's reign are somewhat muddled as to
details, but an interesting description of him has survived, as well
as the account of an incident that sheds light on a little-known
Turkish custom. A contemporary French source describes the
sultan as resembling a Tartar: short and thickset, with broad
face, small eyes, and a big crooked nose. Other chroniclers of
his time thought it worth mentioning that once he bought six
hundred Greek slaves and sacrificed them to his dead father.

That item is seldom mentioned in histories of the Ottoman
Empire, but it does appear to have been an example of Ottoman
practice, not merely the homicidal whim of a tubby little sultan.
Perhaps as a holdover from their distant past as steppe nomads,

Ottomans engaged in human sacrifice to honor the dead. For example, Murad's contemporary, the Byzantine Emperor John, reports that Turkish warriors fallen in battle were buried with the enemies they had killed (with the belief that the dead foes would serve their killers in the next world). But if there weren't any dead enemies around, the Turks bought Christian slaves and made do with them. One might think that the Turks' adoption of Islam would have put an end to these sacrifices, but it seems to have made no difference; possibly the extensive rights that Muslim law allowed slave owners over their infidel human property in fact facilitated them.

It is also clear from the sources that, like his predecessors, Murad continued to shovel soldiers and supplies across the Straits into *Rumeli* — as the Turks called Europe — usually with the help of the Genoese fleet. The Ottoman Empire at this time had not become a naval power, so Christian opportunists helped them out. Booty and slaves — including the boys collected in *devşirme* raids — flowed the other way, to Murad's capital at Brusa in Anatolia. In the last years of the fourteenth century, Murad seems to have concentrated on two projects: gaining control of the little Anatolian Turkish emirates that had somehow stubbornly maintained their independence, and pushing further into Bulgaria, Macedonia, Albania, and Serbia. Both moves succeeded. The fragile coalitions formed against the Turks by various Balkan rulers did not hold; if one of them, such as the Serbian King Lazar in 1386, agreed to Ottoman terms, there was not much hope for the rest.

Still, there were some setbacks for the Turks, including a defeat in Bosnia in 1388. This led in 1389 to the tragic battle of Kosovo, which, curiously, still looms as large in the historical memory of the Serbs as victories do in the memories of other peoples. In this epic struggle on the "Field of Blackbirds," the

Ottoman army faced and defeated the combined forces of Bosnia and of King Lazar of Serbia, who obviously had not been quite reconciled to the Turkish suzerainty over his kingdom that he had accepted three years earlier. In the course of the battle, Murad was killed by a Serb, whereupon the captive King Lazar was executed by the Turks. Murad's son Bayazid, also fighting in the battle, immediately succeeded his father, as Lazar's son Stephen succeeded him. This Turkish victory is considered to have sealed the fate of the Balkans, though many battles remained to be fought and countless lives would yet be lost. Stephen was forced to become an Ottoman vassal and agree to his sister's marriage to Bayazid.[2]

Bayazid the Busy

Bayazid's reign was brief but eventful. Not without reason was he called "the Thunderbolt," because his policy was to decide on things quickly and do them *now*. The independence of those few emirates — some in remote areas of eastern Anatolia — that had remained outside Ottoman control was destroyed, while the campaigns in Rumeli were energetically continued. This whirlwind of a ruler has always been considered one of the great sultans, perhaps even greater than Murad. Certainly he was a great conqueror.

By the last decade of the fourteenth century he was in full control of the Balkans, except for certain areas under Hungarian protection — although he did lead his army across the

---

[2] It would probably be fruitless to investigate the lives of these numerous Christian women forced into marriages with Turks, including that ten-year-old Byzantine princess mentioned in the previous chapter, though I wish some researcher would try. As it is, they disappear almost entirely from history, leaving only a shudder behind them.

Danube to defeat the new Hungarian King Sigismund in Wallachia. The Turkish blitzkrieg also included the annexation of Bulgaria and the blockading of Constantinople; the effectiveness of the latter, however, was hampered by the continued lack of an Ottoman fleet.

Another Failed Crusade

King Sigismund had long been trying to rally the other states of Europe for a new crusade. Historians' reviews of that king's domestic policies may be mixed, but at least he was one of those who realized Europe's peril. He also realized that since he had concluded an alliance with Byzantine Emperor Manuel II, Sultan Bayazid was likely to turn his thunderbolts in the direction of Hungary. In 1396, Sigismund succeeded in assembling a genuine multi-national force to march south against the Turks.

He was fortunate that his project took shape at the time of a truce during the Hundred Years' War between England and France, freeing the knights of both countries for the crusade. The assembled troops of the German, Hungarian, Polish, English, French and other nations, all under the command of a somewhat inexperienced twenty-five-year-old John of Burgundy, marched toward Nicopolis near the mouth of the Danube. Meanwhile, warships of the Knights Hospitaller, Venetians, and Genoese (on the same side, for once) moved into place in the Black Sea. Emperor Manuel II, blockaded in his capital, may have been able at least to help with the costs of the crusade.

The Turks were better-trained and disciplined, and Sigismund knew that only equal discipline and careful planning based on a study of the enemy's military behavior could produce victory. His idea was that the Hungarian infantry should meet the first assault, with the cavalry behind them. Once arrived outside Nicopolis, however, the army had to await the Turks for so long — over two weeks — that discipline broke down, factional quarrels erupted, and many wondered if there would ever be a battle at all. When Bayazid appeared suddenly (as usual) on the scene on September 25, the disorganization of the Westerners was apparent. The French were unwilling to follow Sigismund's wise battle plan; they huffily (one would almost say childishly) assumed that the king wanted all the glory for himself and his army, and charged into the fray, in defiance of the king's advice, far ahead of the main force.

The knights dismounted from their horses to fight their way through the forest of stakes the Turks had set up to deflect cavalry, and succeeded in cutting their way through part of Bayazid's infantry. Having exhausted themselves doing this, they raised their eyes to the crest of the hill in front of them and saw . . . the main Ottoman army of some tens of thousands, including cavalry and chariots, swooping down upon them. The heavily armored French knights were helpless on foot against the attack, and large numbers perished. Sigismund courageously advanced with his foot soldiers, but the knights had got too far ahead and there was no way to save the situation.

The defeat of the crusade was complete, with thousands lying dead or wounded on the battlefield and many others taken captive. Thousands more managed either to reach the ships of the Knights Hospitaller or embark on harrowing journeys to their homes on foot. The following day, the sultan is said to have ordered most of the prisoners executed, except for a few of the more prominent, such as John of Burgundy, who were held for ransom. These nobles were constrained to watch their companions forced to their knees and beheaded. King Sigismund, meanwhile, narrowly escaped capture and made his way to a small ship and the start of a lengthy journey home from the Black Sea through the Straits to the Adriatic. The fleetless Turks were unable to stop him, but as his vessel was going through the Dardanelles they lined up their Christian prisoners on the banks and taunted him to leave his ship and save them.

The only favorable result of the whole melancholy enterprise was that Bayazid was forced to lift the blockade of Constantinople temporarily in order to deal with the crusaders, thus providing a respite for the beleaguered city. Its emperor wrote in an essay that although his life as a young man had been "full of tribulations . . . it might have been foreseen that our future would cause us to look at the past as a time of clear tranquility." From his most un-tranquil capital, where seditious sentiment was growing, Manuel again sent out urgent letters to all the prospects he could think of: the Russian ruler Vasili in Moscow, the pope, and the rulers of the most powerful states of the West. He seems to have received favorable answers from most of them, though most of the help they sent was in the form of money — and not enough of that. What Manuel really needed was troops, and those only the King of France, Charles VI, sent, dispatching 1,200 soldiers under the command of the legendary Boucicaut (real name Jean Meingre), Marshal of France.

The Adventures of Boucicaut

This high-energy knight seems to have had adventures all over the map in the last few decades of the fourteenth century, from Palestine to Lithuania to the Ottoman Empire. To his enemies he must have seemed practically indestructible. He fought with extraordinary bravery in the Crusade of 1396, and was said to have eluded death almost miraculously. Captured by the Turks and then ransomed, he was back in France the next year, all ready to take command of the royal troops and charge off to fight the Turks again.

In 1397, Bayazid, who knew the troop ships were coming, did his utmost to prevent them by renewing the blockade of the Byzantine capital; he was no match for Boucicaut, who slipped through the blockade as he did through most of the dangers and difficulties of his adventurous life, defeating what enemy ships he met and arriving with his men at Constantinople. The blockade could only be partial at this point, given the lack of an Ottoman fleet and the strong fortifications of the harbor on the Black Sea side of the city. Thus the marshal and the emperor were able to make raids on the Turks along the coast and even along the shores of the Black Sea, but were unable to force the lifting of the blockade, which had been in place for most of the previous six years, and was increasingly strangling the city's food supply. Always a man with another plan in his fertile brain, Boucicaut decided to return to France for more help and persuaded Manuel to go with him in order to make a stronger appeal to Europe; they set off for Venice late in 1399. As had his father, Emperor Manuel II then embarked on an extended tour of Europe to beg for help for his people, leaving his nephew John in charge of the government in his absence. He was to be gone over three years, spending several months in Paris, where he was promised more troops, to be led once again by the indefatigable Boucicaut. The emperor then went on to London, where he was promised a great deal of assistance but received none. He returned to Paris for another long and frustrating stay, finally leaving for home with little to show for his efforts except kind words and vague promises. He was, however, to have spectacular good news upon returning to his capital.

The Downfall of Bayazid

Once the dust had settled after the Battle of Nicopolis, the sultan hoped to turn his attention again both to taking the Byzantine capital and punishing the upstart Christian crusaders with another blitzkrieg. No one doubts that this human cannonball would have immediately galloped his army off in both directions, had not one of those divine surprises occurred that saved, at least temporarily, both of Bayazid's targets while removing Bayazid from the scene permanently.

The last decades of the fourteenth century in Central Asia had seen the rise of another great Mongol conqueror, the equal of his predecessors of the previous century who had spread terror and wholesale devastation throughout much of Asia and Eastern Europe. Tamerlane (Timur-the-Lame, from a battle injury) was a civilized, ruthless, and extremely successful Muslim warlord with grand designs on everything from the lands of his fellow Mongols to India and China. He is said to have been responsible for millions of deaths in the lands through which he raged; even given the unreliability of statistics from his time and place, the toll seems to have indeed been enormous. So was the destruction of churches and Christian communities, most of them belonging to the Nestorian, Jacobite, or other sects. In his correspondence with Bayazid he seems to have resented the sultan's assertion of control over some eastern emirates that had previously acknowledged Mongol sovereignty; he also seems to have considered the Seljuq Turks as still the rightful lords of Asia Minor instead of the Ottomans. It may have been such motives as these that triggered his decision to go to war with the Ottoman Empire.

Christopher Dawson has described Tamerlane as "one of the great destroyers in history . . . his career was like a tornado which passed across Asia from the Ganges to the Aegean, leaving ruin behind it." When the Tornado hit the Thunderbolt at Ankara in 1402, the Turks went down to defeat. Bayazid was taken prisoner and died in captivity. Tamerlane, having reversed Bayazid's conquests in Anatolia and temporarily reduced the size of the Ottoman Empire, turned east to harass China a few years later. He was aging, possibly suffering from fever, and the winter of 1407 was bitterly cold. When the Mongols made camp, their frozen leader headed for the fire and, according to one account, began guzzling heated wine (though Gibbon blamed his downfall on "the indiscreet use of iced water") in enormous quantities, trying to get warm. Whether his beverage was hot or cold he was dead shortly thereafter, to the relief of nearly all of his contemporaries.

Leaderless as well as freezing, the Mongols pushed on eastward, leaving their imperium to fragment behind them, and did not again become a serious threat to the Near East or to the West. Some Mongol chiefs in Mesopotamia and elsewhere, however, held onto the territories under their rule, and for some time to come remained capable of making trouble for the sultans by supporting disaffected emirs on the eastern border of Anatolia. We will see one example of this later on.

Back in the Turkish realm, as the sons of Bayazid bickered over the succession to his throne and the Anatolian emirates reasserted their freedom from Ottoman control once again, the Ottoman Empire entered a period of instability that lasted until 1425. Now, if ever, the West might have taken advantage of the Turks' weakness to liberate at least some of their Christian conquests. The usual preoccupation with national rivalries and domestic problems got in the way again, however, and the twenty-three-year window of opportunity closed. The great Western powers had spent it wrangling with each other, and the Hundred Years' War dragged on; Marshal Boucicaut nearly died once again fighting in the Battle of Agincourt in 1415, but was dragged out from under a pile of other wounded and dead and made a prisoner by the English. The French hero who was one of Byzantium's greatest friends finally died for good in England in 1421, at the age of sixty-five. Meanwhile, the maritime states that alternately traded and fought with the Turks continued to trade and (occasionally) fight with them, while the Catholic Church was still trying to find a way to end the tiresome Great Schism that had gone on far too long. It began to seem as though the Turks were there to stay: just another part of the international scene.

Byzantine Desperation

The clock of history was ticking off the last nine years of life for Constantinople, and the Turks were making new inroads into the greatly reduced territory still left to Byzantium. They mounted an attack on Constantinople in 1422, a sort of dress rehearsal for the eventual conquest to come; it was unsuccessful but profoundly unsettling to the city's inhabitants, and once again an emperor (John VIII, now Manuel's co-emperor,) spent several months traveling to Hungary and Italy in a futile search for aid. Manuel died in 1425, paralyzed and worn out with work and anxiety; he was greatly mourned.

The Ottomans now turned on Greece, capturing Thessalonica in 1430. The results for the ancient Macedonian city were grim: the murder of citizens of all ages and conditions, looting, destruction, and the turning of churches into mosques. With the apparent goal of imposing both Islam and "Turkishness" upon it, Sultan Mehemmed II practiced forced deportation in addition to the removal of large numbers of Greek boys from the city by means of the *devşirme*. Fewer Greeks in the city, more Turks, and at least some conversions of Christians to the Muslim religion, he thought, would turn this jewel of the Eastern Empire into a jewel of the Ottoman Empire. The policy failed to work. Somehow, for most of the rest of the century, the Christians of Thessalonica generally managed to maintain their majority. Following the expulsion of the Jews of Spain in 1492, however, Sultan Bayazid II had the idea of not only giving them refuge within his empire but of settling them all in Thessalonica. The result was that the city did not again have a Christian majority until after its liberation from the Turks in 1912.

The Union of Florence

Within the Church, the end of the first quarter of the fifteenth century saw the Great Schism at last resolved. However, the council that had been the vehicle for its resolution then puffed itself up with the assertion that its authority was higher than that of the popes. That issue of Conciliarism then had to be dealt with, as did the Hussite Wars touched off in Bohemia by the execution of the heretic John Hus. And at long last, in the 1430s, the increasingly desperate political and religious leaders of Byzantium became seriously committed to meeting with Roman authorities. This historic gathering began at Ferrara but soon moved, for a number of practical reasons, and is now known as the Council of Florence. To it came the new emperor of Byzantium, John VIII, his Patriarch, and a number of Greek bishops; the Archbishop of Kiev also came, along with other Orthodox clergy.

Given the desperate situation of his shrinking realm, it is natural that John VIII would have expected more than theology to be discussed at the council. He wanted the Union; he also urgently needed a concerted Western campaign against the Turks, who were after all the common enemy of East and West. But the debates, which went on for months, were purely theological and mainly concerned with the *filioque* question — whether the Holy Spirit proceeds from the Father only or from the Father and the Son — and with the issue of papal jurisdiction. Indeed, the Orthodox objected to the fact that the West had made an addition (the words, "and the Son") to the Creed, more than to the doctrine itself, and had long demanded conciliar consideration of the point. The historic declaration of reunion of the Latin and Orthodox Churches was signed in 1439, and now, surely, would come the great crusade that would finally liberate Byzantium and the Balkans from the Turkish yoke.

But the time when a pope could make a plea to Europe for military action and receive a whole-hearted response seemed to have passed. As Aeneas Sylvius, the future Pope Pius II, noted in his diary, the powerful nations of the West were too secularized, too concerned with their own wars, to cooperate as members of the body of Christendom. In any case, no energetic preaching of crusade was heard at the council. A few years later, however, papal preaching would manage to inspire another heroic effort, albeit a pitifully small one.

The Crusade of Varna

The loss of the great Macedonian city of Thessalonica was a shock both to the West and to the anguished residents of Constantinople, surely the next large target on the sultan's list. Following the Union of Florence between the Catholic and Orthodox Churches, Pope Eugenius IV preached a new crusade that brought together twenty-five thousand Hungarians, Poles, and Rumanians under the command of Vladislav V, the young king of both Poland and Hungary, the Serb leader George

Brankovic, and the great Hungarian hero Janos Hunyadi. This accomplished soldier had risen to a position of great prominence, had defeated the Turks in Transylvania in 1442, and talked the king into a bold campaign against them in the Balkans the following year. He was a romantic figure in his silver armor, guarding the southern frontier of Hungary and repelling Turkish raids.

In 1443, then, the crusading army was marching south through Serbia, liberating town after town from their Ottoman garrisons — all of the towns, in fact, on the road between the Danube and Sofija, in modern Bulgaria. Within the towns, they converted (or reconverted) the mosques into churches, aided by Bulgarians who provided supplies and support. On they went toward Adrianople, considerably encouraged. One reason for their encouragement was the totally unexpected arrival on the scene of a new champion.

A New Christian Champion

George Castriot was the son of John Castriot, ruler of Epirus, a region on the border between Greece and Albania. In 1423, John had been forced by the Turks to relinquish his four young sons to Murad II as hostages. At the sultan's court, the boys seem to have been forcibly converted to Islam and trained, like so many kidnapped Christian boys, to serve the Turkish ruler. The fate of the older boys is unknown; they disappear from the records and may have been killed. The youngest, George, then about nineteen, survived and showed a great aptitude for warfare. He soon rose to become one of the finest of the Ottoman officers. His stature, skill, and bravery were such that he was known as *Iskander beg*, or Skanderbeg, probably an allusion to Alexander the Great.

Back in Albania, the Turks had brought disaster. Their campaigns of the early 1430s had resulted in the loss of many fortresses and a great deal of land to new Ottoman fief-holders from Anatolia and a number of tame Albanians, some of whom were willing to become Muslim. The Castriots, George's family, were among those who lost the most in land and resources. Shortly thereafter, spurred on by rumors of the sultan's death, revolt against the Turks spread throughout Albania. The patriots won a number of battles with the armies sent against them, and Skanderbeg's relatives are said to have sent word to him to return home and help them. He was then serving with the Ottoman army in Asia Minor, and whether he got the message or not, he did not come.

Murad II was not dead after all, however, and in 1436 an enormous Ottoman army invaded Albania, crushing the revolt with savage massacres and leaving pyramids of skulls behind it. Submissive Albanian chiefs were allowed to keep at least part of their lands, though more of their sons were taken hostage as a guarantee of their compliance. And still Skanderbeg did not return. It was the Crusade of Varna that finally brought him into the fray.

It may have been the plight of his family and the loss of their lands that angered John Castriot's son and determined him to turn against the Turks, or he may have been planning to revolt for some time and for other reasons. In any case, the sultan himself furnished the opportunity by sending Skanderbeg and his Ottoman army against the crusaders at Nis in 1443. Accounts of what happened next vary. One story has Skanderbeg, with three hundred other Albanians loyal to him, approaching the forces of Janos Hunyadi and, suddenly proclaiming his Christianity, switching sides to join the Hungarians in the defeat of the Turks. Another version has it that he simply deserted with his men during the battle. He must have thought out his preparations carefully in advance, since he was equipped with forged papers that allowed him to pass as the new governor of an Albanian town. Once in control of the town, he announced that he was a Christian and began to reverse the forced Islamization that the Turks had been imposing on the region. He is said to have gone to the extreme of ordering the execution of those who refused to convert to Christianity.

Skanderbeg then liberated his family's lands and married the daughter of another powerful family, now also in rebellion against the Turks. In 1444 he called a conference of all the Albanian chiefs and the Venetians, who had interests in the area, in order to forge a league to fight against the Turks. The Albanians willingly agreed and furnished soldiers for the cause; they were now united under an Albanian leader for the first time in their history. The Ottomans, alarmed at the situation, attacked in force in the spring of 1444. Skanderbeg, however, had spies who warned him in advance of when and where the assault would occur and the Albanians, skilled in mountain fighting and ambushes and under a leader who knew the Turkish military inside out, easily defeated the enemy in June.

Meanwhile, the crusaders' campaigns of 1442 and 1443 had succeeded so well that the Turks were alarmed. The harrowing progress of the army across the Balkan Mountains in winter was made even more difficult as the Turks blocked the passes with stones and flooded the passes with water, turning the paths and mountainsides into sheets of ice. (Kinross calls this march of the crusaders "a military feat seldom paralleled in history.") After a victory on Christmas Day, 1443, bad weather made Hunyadi decide to retreat temporarily to Hungary. The exhausted, half-frozen, and starving men marched into Buda with their young king on foot at their head, singing Christmas carols and carrying captured Turkish banners. They received a tumultuous welcome as they proceeded to the cathedral to give heartfelt thanks to God for their victorious campaign and safe return. Following a well-deserved rest, they planned to resume the crusade in the spring.

The Defection of Serbia

Meanwhile, Murad not only had this unexpected European feistiness to cope with, but was also faced with a revolt by the Emirate of Karamania in central Anatolia. Relations between the Ottoman state and Karamania seem to have been sour for some time. It appears that the Venetians, and perhaps the Hungarians, had attempted in the 1430s to establish relations with disaffected rulers of Asia Minor, with whom they hoped to make common cause. They seem to have succeeded with Karamania, and this little thorn in Murad's side (or rather in his rear, as he fought the crusaders in Europe) was now raiding the sultan's Anatolian territories.

A harried Murad decided to approach George Brankovic, ruler of Serbia and probably the weakest link of the crusading coalition. Serbia's independence and aggrandizement were George's top priority, and took precedence over the common effort. He happily agreed to make peace with the Turks, receiving in return a guarantee that Serbia, previously liberated by the crusaders, would remain unoccupied by the Turks and have much of its lost territory restored. He also accepted Turkish suzerainty and agreed to a stiff tribute. He had some years earlier, under pressure, given his daughter to Murad as a wife; his two sons, whom the sultan had had blinded, were now restored to their father.

Once Brankovic had accepted peace with the Turks, representatives of the remaining leaders of the crusade agreed to a

ten-year peace with the Turks, but it is not clear that this decision was ever accepted by King Vladislav or Janos Hunyadi. Its
terms included the liberation of Serbia from Ottoman control,
which Murad had used to gain the Serb ruler's abandonment of
the crusade, but the peace also interfered with the planning of
the rest of the crusade, and Cardinal Cesarini, the papal legate,
opposed it. A fleet was already en route to support the Christian army, unbeknownst to the crusaders, and the victories of
1442 and 1443 gave promise of further success. The Cardinal's
advice was that the king should not ratify the truce, leaving the
Christian leaders free to lead their troops against the Ottoman
army once again.

An enraged Murad II confronted the crusaders outside Varna
on November 10, 1444, and defeated them completely. George
Brankovic had again declared neutrality before the battle, since
he was satisfied with the peace treaty that had liberated Serbia
and perhaps disapproved of its repudiation by the other crusaders; he had gone so far as to refuse the crusaders' passage
through Serbia, and had possibly even warned the sultan that
the Christians were coming. King Vladislav died in the battle,
Cardinal Cesarini was murdered as he fled, and Hunyadi himself
narrowly escaped alive. He bravely tried again for victory in
1448, at the second battle of Kosovo, but was again defeated,
though Skanderbeg managed a victory over the Turks at roughly
the same time. These engagements were the last spark of the
West's feeble collective resistance to the Ottoman jihad in the
Balkans; although the great Christian champions such as Skanderbeg and Hunyadi continued to fight for the Christian cause
until their deaths, Constantinople was now truly doomed.

Skanderbeg's Albania

Within Albania, Skanderbeg had more than the Turks to worry about. The Venetians, who controlled towns and ports throughout the Balkans, including Albania, often proved so duplicitous in their disputes with the Albanian ruler that Machiavelli could have taken lessons from them. In 1447, for example, because of a dispute over the town of Danj, the Venetians offered a reward for Skanderbeg's assassination, and urged the Turks to attack Albania again. In 1449 and 1450 the sultan himself led massive Turkish assaults on Albania. Hard pressed, Skanderbeg was forced in 1449 to accept Ottoman suzerainty and pay tribute, though he soon reasserted Albanian independence and refused payment. During these campaigns, the Turks were buying supplies from the Venetians, who were supposedly then at peace with Albania. Even during the great Ottoman onslaught of 1450, when an army of perhaps one hundred thousand fell upon Albania, Venice refused to aid to the defenders. In a series of brilliant moves, the undaunted Skanderbeg took to the mountains and launched lightning attacks on the Turkish forces, causing great damage and heavy casualties to the enemy, who were unable even to take the town they had besieged at the start of the campaign; they finally withdrew from the country.

With no prospects of help from Venice, Skanderbeg made an alliance with Naples that brought him a modest number of troops, just in time to meet (and defeat) another Turkish attack in 1452. Venice was obviously untrustworthy, but there were also Albanians from some of the powerful families who supported either the Turks or the Venetians, for territorial or other advantages. The Catholic Church was able to use its influence, beginning in 1452, to promote a peace settlement between the rebels and Skanderbeg; at the same time, the Ottomans were now preoccupied with their plans for Constantinople, and so Albania had a short period of peace.

The later exploits of both Hunyadi and Skanderbeg we will witness in the next chapter, on the other side of the great cataclysm of 1453.

MAIN WORKS CONSULTED

Bolton, Andrew G., M.D., editor. *The Legacy of Jihad.*

The Cambridge Medieval History.

Carroll, Warren H. *A History of Christendom.* The author's argument that the crusaders of Varna did not ratify the truce with the Turks is found on pp. 553–54.

Dawson, Christopher, editor. *The Mongol Mission.*

Fine, John V. A., Jr. *The Late Medieval Balkans.*

Hughes, Philip, Msgr. *The Church in Crisis.*

Kinross, Lord. *The Ottoman Empire.*

Pastor, Ludwig von. *History of the Popes*, vol. II.

Pius II, Pope. *Memoirs of a Renaissance Pope.*

Vasiliev, A. A. *History of the Byzantine Empire*, vol. II.

Vryonis, Speros, Jr. *The Decline of Medieval Hellenism.* This is the source for information about human sacrifice among the Turks.

Ye'or, Bat. *The Decline of Eastern Christianity Under Islam.*

Three

The City Falls and the Heroes Die

The mid-fifteenth century brought a breathing space to the embattled Turkish targets in Eastern Europe and the Aegean Sea, but it was very brief. By the dawn of the year 1453, everyone knew that Byzantium's final agony, one of the most tragic scenes in the drama of the Ottomans, was about to begin.

Byzantine Anti-Catholicism Isolates the East

The ruler of the Turks in 1453 was twenty-one-year-old Mehemmed II, who had succeeded to the throne on the death of his father Murad II in 1451. Having disposed of an infant rival by having him killed — the usual method employed by new sultans for dealing with the many candidates that harems tended to produce — he turned his attention to the main task of his reign: the taking of the Byzantine capital.

At this point the Ottoman Empire consisted of two parts: one was the original Anatolian heartland of the Ottomans with its capital at Brusa in Anatolia, strongly linked to the Islamic Middle East and traditional Sunni Muslim ways, and the other was the European area of Rumelia, with its capital at Adrianople. Rumelia was a land of the frontier and of Muslim adventurers. Their new mentality and way of life distanced them somewhat

from their Anatolian relatives; Rumelia was also the land of the
dervishes, with their unorthodox mysticism and theology. The
sultans considered a Turkish Constantinople desirable for many
reasons, not least of which was that it might bring both regions
of the Ottoman Empire into greater unity and harmony.

Mehemmed thus started work on the final siege of Constantinople as soon as he became sultan. He began by build-
ing two large fortresses on either side of the Bosphorus to the
northeast of the city, to cut it off from the Black Sea. Emperor
Constantine XI sent urgent requests for help to Rome, promising recognition of the Union of Florence. At the papal court,
opinion was somewhat divided, with some hardliners arguing
that the Greeks remained on the whole heretics and schismatics
and were therefore undeserving of aid.

The more charitable view prevailed, however, and in May
1452 Cardinal Isidore, formerly a Greek delegate to the Council
of Florence who had there accepted Catholicism, was sent to
Constantinople as papal legate. With him went two hundred
troops, perhaps a token of what the pope hoped to raise from the
European powers. The pope also sent funds to help fortify the
walls of Galata, on the north shore of the city's harbor known
as the Golden Horn. Cardinal Isidore found the majority of the
Byzantines as fanatically opposed to union as ever, which made
a mockery of the ceremony in celebration of the Union that was
held in Hagia Sophia in December 1452 and included prayers for
the pope.

This extreme hostility on the part of the Byzantines and (as we
shall see) the masses of Orthodox in the Balkans and Greece, is
somewhat puzzling. Time and time again we are told in accounts
of the period that it was "the people" who were so attached
to their leavened bread for Communion, the doctrine that the

Holy Spirit proceeds only from the Father, and the authority of their patriarchs over that of the pope. I find it hard to believe that, on their own, ordinary people would become so exercised over what goes on in the Trinity. I can better understand their attachment to the more tangible issue of leavened bread, but that was permitted under the terms of the Union and should have been a non-issue after the Council of Florence. As for the authority of the Roman pontiffs, ordinary people had little direct experience of any kind with it, since their local religious authorities remained the same.

The only historical comparison I can think of for this inveterate hostility to Rome is the implacable antagonism of the post-Reformation English to the Catholic Church. And the only way I can account — on the natural level at least — for the seemingly spontaneous popular hatred of Catholicism in England is by referring to the clever use, on the part of the Protestant political elite, of constant propaganda that appealed to base passions: ambitious and opportunistic leaders appealed to cultural differences, national autonomy, and old historical grudges to promote English antagonism to Rome. Similar methods were used to encourage Orthodox hostility to Catholicism; besides theological grievances, much was made of resentment against the Latin conquest of Constantinople in 1204 (Byzantine atrocities against Latins were ignored) and of the temporary Western rule over much of the empire that had resulted.[3] Atrocities are hard to erase from local memory, and that was certainly the case with the citizens of Constantinople whose ancestors and possessions had perished in 1204.

---

[3] On this point, there may be a historical parallel with the attitude of the Irish to Cromwell's conquest of Ireland, particularly the city of Drogheda.

Opponents of union played upon such historical grievances from the pulpit, Sunday after Sunday, and frequently during the week by other means. In this perspective, "the people" screaming, "Better the turban than the tiara!" would be far less culpable, as least in the majority of cases, than the unreconciled preachers who fed them their lines. Whether this is the true interpretation of Orthodox hostility I don't know, but it would seem to be at least a partial explanation. Like any prejudice, a close-minded bias against Catholicism promoted among the populace for generations enters deeply into the psyche and becomes second nature — an automatic reaction upon which those who profess it rarely reflect. They "know" what they have always been told.

Despite the rancor of his religious establishment, Emperor Constantine XI firmly proclaimed the Union of the Churches. His clergy, on the other hand, condemned those who favored union and are said to have refused absolution to those who had been present at the celebration in Hagia Sophia, and instructed the sick to die without the sacraments if the only choice was to receive them from a "uniate" priest. When incidents such as this — and there were many — became known in Europe, it is understandable that they tended to prejudice Catholic nations against sending men to die for people who seemed to have nothing but contempt for them. And so, once again, attempts by Constantine and the papacy to rally support were largely in vain. There was no charismatic Marshal Boucicaut around to raise an army and save the city. Besides the papacy, only the Kingdom of Naples, Venice, and Genoa prepared to send aid, and with most of the Italians it was out of vested commercial interests rather than religious or political commitment.

The Great Siege of Constantinople

Mehemmed did not attack Constantinople as soon as he had built those fortresses. A careful planner, he wanted to be sure that no help could come from the Byzantine possessions in Greece still ruled by members of the imperial family. He therefore, in 1452, attacked the Morea — the Peloponnese (southern peninsula of Greece). Ottoman troops engaged in large-scale plundering and once again reduced the population and its rulers to acknowledging Ottoman suzerainty, though the Greek defenders achieved some local victories. It was not the last time the Morea would suffer Turkish oppression, but its spirit was not broken. It would be from there that the final — and finally successful — revolt of the Greeks against the Turks would begin in 1821.

Mopping up a few more pockets of uncooperative or untrustworthy citizens, Mehemmed proceeded to attack Constantinople in earnest on April 6 or 7, 1453. The Turkish army was eighty thousand strong according to some sources; however many of them there were, it was a lot. The defenders, on the other hand, had only about two thousand soldiers and perhaps an equal number of other citizens capable of bearing arms. There were also seven hundred Genoese soldiers, Venetians, and other resident foreigners, but it all added up to a pitifully small number. As for the promised ships from the West, most of them never arrived or came too late. The strength of the city was in the great chain and walls that protected the harbor and the even more massive walls on the west side that had never, in the thousand years of its history, been breached. They would be this time.

Unbeknown to the defenders, Mehemmed had acquired a super weapon in the form of a cannon nearly thirty feet long, capable of blowing holes in anything with its half-ton shot.

For six weeks, the great cannon fired at the great walls. Seven shots a day seems to have been its limit; hundreds of men and dozens of oxen were required to move it, and even then it sometimes slipped in the mud or rolled off its carriage. Still, the devastation it produced was unlike anything previously seen in siege warfare. Walls that had stood for a thousand years crumbled into dust where the shots struck, their defenders pulverized with them.

The Turks did not have it all their own way, though, especially in the early days of the assault. The three galleys Pope Nicholas had hired from Genoa made it through the Straits and nearly reached the city, along with a Byzantine supply ship. They were seen by both Turks and defenders, and an all-day battle resulted between the tiny group of Christian vessels and the Turkish fleet — such as it was. Fortunately the Turks were still not very good at seamanship or shipbuilding, and the wind was against them in the beginning. The Christian ships were better built, better manned, and gaining the upper hand when the wind suddenly dropped and the current began to pull them toward the other side of the Bosphorus, where Mehemmed himself was on the shore loudly urging his sailors on. Each of the Christian ships found itself surrounded by numerous Turkish vessels, and still they held out. The sailors on the Byzantine supply ship were able to make good use of their incendiary arsenal, the "Greek fire" that had so astonished Westerners in the days of the Crusades. Genoese sailors, in better armor than the Turks, hurled missiles down on the enemy from their taller ships, and surrounded the supply ship to protect it as it ran low on ammunition. The sun was setting and fresh Ottoman ships had been sent into the fray when the wind shifted again, and the Christian ships made it to safety.

The sultan was beside himself with fury. One of his advisors reported that his judgment was already being questioned. Not daring to execute his chief admiral, as he probably would have dearly loved to do, Mehemmed had him beaten and publicly humiliated as a coward and traitor, confiscated his property, and sent him into exile somewhere or other. It was now the end of May, and still the city held. One Turkish stratagem after another was countered by the defenders: attempts to tunnel under the walls were foiled by the defenders' flooding of some of the tunnels and the capture of a number of tunnel-makers who revealed the location of the rest of them. A Venetian vessel that had been sent out to seek help some time earlier slipped back into the city. The news it brought was that there was no help to be had, but the Turks didn't know that. Rumors spread among them that a major Christian fleet was on the way, and the Hungarians informed the sultan, ominously, that a change in their regency had nullified the armistice they'd had with him. There was more murmuring against the Ottoman ruler, and his grand vizier advised abandoning the assault. On May 25, Mehemmed actually offered to raise the siege in return for a sum that proved too large for the Byzantine treasury; surrender was out of the question, so the siege continued.

Within the city, supplies were low, food limited, and the defenders exhausted; even the emperor fainted once during a council meeting. Reports of unexplained phenomena, witnessed by both Christians and Turks, abounded: mysterious lights in the distance that misled the Turks into thinking another Christian force had arrived; other lights playing about the spire of Hagia Sophia, witnessed by both Turks and Greeks. Mehemmed was too confident of success, or perhaps too unwilling to face the consequences of failure, to give up the siege, and decided to make a final assault with everything he had. The Byzantines, seeing the signs of Turkish preparation and probably receiving accurate intelligence reports, knew it was coming. On the night before the city's fall, both Catholic and Orthodox clergy, Cardinal Isidore and all who could be spared from the defense, flooded into the great cathedral. People confessed and received Communion from the priests of both Churches.

The City Finally Falls

The end began shortly before dawn on May 29; there was no stopping the flood of Janissaries and other troops pouring through the great holes their cannon had made in the walls, though the defenders died trying to do so. Emperor Constantine fought in the imperial purple until he realized the last moments of the Christian life of his city were at hand. Then he tore off the royal robe and plunged into battle as an ordinary foot soldier. As emperor, his life would have been spared; as an anonymous soldier, he could die for his people and his Faith — which is what he did.

Most accounts state that the city was given over to looting by the army for three days before the commander was to enter, as stipulated in Islamic law; a few say Mehemmed entered the city on the first day and restored order. Whether it was three days or one, the civilian population endured pillage, destruction, and slaughter by the Ottoman troops that were nothing short of infernal. Turkish soldiers destroyed cultural treasures, tore up or sold off valuable books both sacred and secular books, and burned holy images in fires to cook their food. A crucifix was carried about topped with a janissary cap while the Turks jeered, "Behold the God of the Christians."

Thousands had flocked into Hagia Sophia to implore a miracle of protection from God and Our Lady, and Mass was being said when the troops broke in. By the time they reached the church, the idea of how much more profitable slaves were than corpses seems to have occurred to many of the soldiers; the result was that most of the people were tied together and taken to the soldiers' barracks. Their unenviable fate — the harem, the beds of soldiers, or the slave market — was that of countless thousands of others in the course of the Turkish jihad. Cardinal Isidore was among those sold as slaves, but was fortunately soon recognized by a Westerner, purchased, and liberated. Hagia Sophia itself was turned into a mosque, as were other churches. One of them eventually became an Ottoman historical museum, something the Communists also liked to do with churches.

Over the centuries, more and more places of worship were lost to the Orthodox until finally they were left with only one church in the city. In the sixteenth century, an Ottoman historian exulted,

> Through the noble efforts of the Mohammedan sultan, for the evil-voiced clash of the bells of the shameless misbelievers was substituted the Moslem call to prayer . . . and the ears of the people of the *Djihad* were filled with the melody. . . . The churches which were within the city were emptied of their vile idols, and cleansed from their filthy and idolatrous impurities; and by the defacement of their images and the erection of the Islamic *mihrabs* and pulpits, many monasteries and chapels became the envy of the Gardens of Paradise. The temples of the misbelievers were turned into the mosques of the pious, and the rays of the light of Islam drove away the hosts of darkness from the place so long the abode of the despicable infidels, and the streaks of the dawn of the Faith dispelled the lurid darkness of oppression, for the word, irresistible as destiny, of the fortunate sultan became supreme in the governance of this new dominion. . . .

Soon after the fall of the city, with the Latin patriarch captured, the clergy elected the learned Gennadius Scolarius, who had accompanied his emperor to the Council of Florence and supported the Union. He had subsequently gone over to the anti-Unionist side and now strongly opposed what he had earlier favored. The sultan approved of his election, invested him with the patriarchal insignia, and made him the head of the national churches elsewhere in the former Byzantine Empire as well. Those churches thus ceased to have an independent existence for a considerable period, and were under the control of a man who could almost be called a Turkish sympathizer. At all costs, the Ottomans wanted to prevent any rapprochement with Catholicism, identified as it was with the enemy West, and therefore they greatly increased the power of the patriarch as a counterweight to Rome. The Ottomans thus appeared as the patrons and protectors of Orthodoxy, and those who had clamored for the turban instead of the tiara felt vindicated. Gennadius was wont to have cozy chats with the sultan about religion, and together they drew up statements of common principles and comparisons of Islam and Christianity as a sort of academic exercise.

The huge number of captives taken — the figures of fifty to sixty thousand are mentioned in the sources, most slated for deportation or slavery — must be understood to include primarily the fit, the useful, the attractive. A contemporary historian, Ducas, who visited Constantinople and interviewed eyewitnesses soon after its fall, has described what happened to those who did not make the grade:

> They [the Turks] slew mercilessly all the elderly, both men and women, in [their] homes, who were not able to leave their homes because of illness or old age. The newborn infants were thrown into the streets. . . . And as many of the aristocrats and nobles of the officials of the palace that he [the sultan] ransomed . . . he executed them. He selected their wives and children, the beautiful

daughters and shapely youths and turned them over to the head eunuch to guard them. . . . And the entire city was to be seen in the tents of the army, and the city lay deserted, naked, mute, having neither form nor beauty.

We have already seen, in chapter one, this cruel practice of slaying the unfit or "useless" in the earlier period of Muslim history.

A legend says that the priest saying Mass in Hagia Sophia was holding the Blessed Sacrament in his hands at the time of the Turks' entrance into the church. Miraculously, the wall before him opened and he passed through; when the great structure is again a Christian church, he will emerge and finish his Mass.

Aftermath of the Fall

Mehemmed II was one for settling scores. He had already dealt with the under-performing admiral, and now his grand vizier, who had been critical of the whole enterprise and whose loyalty the sultan had long suspected, was beheaded. The Grand Duke Lukas Notaras, Constantine's prime minister, had been the source of the much-quoted statement to the effect that he would prefer to see the Turkish turban in the city rather than the Roman tiara. Following the Ottoman victory, the sultan seems to have been well disposed to him at first, and may have seen him as a go-between in dealing with his new Greek subjects. He certainly needed such a highly placed intermediary, since the emperor was dead and the Patriarch had left for Rome.

What eventually soured their relations is unclear; perhaps Notaras was kindly invited to welcome the turban by converting to Islam, and declined the invitation. Another story implies that the depraved sultan wanted Notaras to turn over his fourteen-year-old son for his pleasure and that the father refused. In any case, he, his son and son-in-law were beheaded by order of the sultan. Poor Notaras certainly got the wish he had expressed, though no doubt not precisely in the way he meant it.

During this time many saved themselves, as well as their possessions and their status, by converting to Islam, even though their families often remained Christian. With their connections in both worlds, these renegades became essential to Ottoman governance, as they had earlier been to Arab regimes. Bat Ye'or, in *The Decline of Eastern Christianity Under Islam*, describes the workings of the system:

> The retention of power by the Islamized Christian nobility . . . provided continuity, guaranteed the transition from the Christian state to the Muslim state, and ensured the transfer of technology and administrative skills. . . . In fact, without these relationships, the Arabs and Turks could not have ruled the conquered Christian peoples or remained on their territory.

Possibly some of the collaborators salved their consciences with the thought that they were able to moderate, to a certain extent, the measures taken against their people by the government. The fact remains that they were of vital assistance to the government as it consolidated power over the Christians: just as collaborators with Communism would be in twentieth-century Eastern Europe.

The Turks put the Greek Orthodox patriarch in charge of all the Orthodox in the empire, and as I have mentioned, the Slavic national churches were suppressed. Here again there was collaboration; here again it would be interesting to compare the situation of the Greek Church under the Turks with that of the Russian Orthodox Church under Communism. Religious schismatics were often more opposed to their fellow Christians than to the Turks, and only too willing to cooperate with the

Ottoman masters against their ecclesiastical enemies; the Turks were happy to oblige them (divide and conquer has ever been a useful principle for rulers.) Thus several varieties of traitors and collaborators began to surface as the noise of battle ceased within the city, and the transition from the ancient empire of Constantine the Great to the Ottoman Empire of Mehemmed II — something of a comedown, to say the least — was already underway. Combined with the usual mass deportations of Christians and the settlement of Turks and Muslim converts in their place, as well as the possibility for Muslim men of possessing four wives, any number of concubines, and therefore numerous children, the spiritual, demographic, and psychological situation of the tattered Christian remnants of Byzantium was eroded, and the surviving Christians were gradually reduced to the beleaguered minority they are now.

The Turks Move on to Belgrade

The fall of Constantinople into their hands galvanized the Ottomans with new zeal and energy; their Jihad had so far succeeded spectacularly — surely a sign of the favor of Allah. And Allah did not intend them to stop with Constantinople, did he? Mehemmed saw himself as a world conqueror; he was the grand heir to the Roman and Greek emperors, not to mention the great rulers of Asia, and of course he was a *ghazi* — one of those now legendary warriors for Islam — and Allah's instrument. If New Rome was now his, why not old Rome? The dust had hardly settled in the half-ruined city when the next stage in the invasion of the West began. We shall be following the Ottoman army's progress through the Balkans and Greece in more detail in the following chapter, but one Balkan battle belongs here — at this point we can certainly use a Christian victory to fortify us for the next grimness.

The shock of the catastrophe rippled through the West, causing consternation as far as England, where it may have played a role in bringing on the mysterious illness, perhaps a nervous breakdown, of the holy King Henry VI in 1453. According to the memoirs of the humanist scholar Aeneas Sylvius, who would ascend the papal throne as Pope Pius II in 1458, Pope Nicholas V and the Holy Roman Emperor Frederick III were both widely blamed for not having done more to prevent the cataclysm. In 1454, the emperor called a meeting at which Aeneas spoke persuasively about the need for a new crusade and the assembly voted unanimously in favor of it. Arrangements were being made by the various states about the numbers and types of forces to be provided, when Pope Nicholas suddenly died in March of the following year and the project came to nothing. The next pope, Callistus III, tried to revive support for the crusade, with mixed results.

The country in greatest danger from the Turkish advance into the Balkans was Hungary, which at that time was much larger than it is today and extended as far south as Belgrade, at the junction of the Sava and the Danube rivers. Apparently out of rivalry with the Hungarian king and unwilling to see him benefit from German help, the emperor did nothing to protect Hungary, while German bishops and others grumbled about the tax the pope tried to collect to finance the war effort. Once again international squabbles interfered with support for the crusade from other states. England and France were still at war; maritime powers distrusted each other too much to send many ships away from home; Portugal seems to have sent out a fleet and then called it back. The usual.

Meanwhile Mehemmed II was on the move, and once more things were going his way. In the very year of the fall of Constantinople, two rebellions in the Morea threw the area into turmoil. One involved Albanian immigrants who were unhappy with their Greek ruler, and the other a would-be usurper and his supporters. Incredibly, both groups of rebels appealed to Mehemmed. After his nasty experiences in Albania with the forces of Skanderbeg, Mehemmed was anxious to put down the Morean Albanians, and his troops were already on the spot by the end of 1453. The rebellions were easily crushed, and the rulers restored, saddled with heavy bills for tribute. The rulers of other parts of the Morea also asked to become the sultan's vassals — they knew the winning side when they saw it. The Morea was not yet completely pacified but it was sufficiently subdued for the sultan to move on.

Mehemmed's next target was Serbia, even though his Serb vassals had compliantly furnished troops for the attack on Constantinople. The sultan nevertheless refused to renew his treaty with them and began to raid the country; as usual, it was the ordinary people who suffered most from the Turkish attacks. Large numbers of the enslaved were taken east and settled in the ruins of the depopulated Byzantine capital. By 1455, a major Turkish assault was sweeping most of the rest of Serbia into Ottoman hands, and the army continued north to take over Belgrade — at least that was the plan.

If Belgrade fell, the great Hungarian Plain and all of southeastern Europe would be open to the Muslim armies, but consultations among the Christians about what to do showed once again that they could agree on very little. Hungarian lords were divided on whether to fight or fall back and make a stand someplace else. The feudal magnates were reluctant to commit troops to a common effort, and the Hungarian king seemed to be of two minds. He had sense enough, however, to appoint Janos Hunyadi commander-in-chief of the Hungarian army. Since we last met Hunyadi fighting at Varna, Kosovo, and elsewhere in chapter three, he had been multi-tasking with amazing energy. For a time he was in charge of the royal revenues, mediator of dynastic disputes, and regent of Hungary — as well as a fighter against domestic enemies of the throne and, of course, the Turks. Like Skanderbeg, this great warrior must have seemed to the Turks to be everywhere at once. He recaptured fortresses that had fallen to them, relieved besieged towns, and repelled several Turkish attacks — in one instance the enemy simply fled in panic at his coming. Then he went to the aid of Belgrade.

The historian J. B. Bury has written, "The siege lasted for three weeks in July, 1456, and hardly has a more brilliant feat been achieved in the course of the struggles between Europe and the Ottoman Turks than the relief of Belgrade by John Hunyadi and his Magyar army." The army that Hunyadi managed to scrape together was pitifully small and untrained. Pope Callistus had sent a papal legate to try to rally support for the cause, and issued a bull calling Christendom to prayer, penance, and fasting. Plague had struck Rome but he refused to flee; as he told an ambassador, the Turks had lost thousands to the plague but that did not cause the sultan to stop his campaign.

The sultan saw no reason why Belgrade should not easily fall, Hunyadi or no Hunyadi. There was, however, someone else besides Hunyadi to reckon with, and he was a saint. The combination of St. John Capistrano and Janos Hunyadi turned out to be unbeatable, even by Allah's instrument in person. Traveling round Hungary, the great Italian preacher galvanized into action those who heard him speak. St. John himself had been at first discouraged by the response to his impassioned appeals, but one day at Mass he saw in a vision an arrow with the words, "Fear not, John. Go down quickly. In the power of my name and of the Holy Cross thou wilt conquer the Turks." He spoke of this vision in his sermons, and his new confidence was infectious. Thousands of peasants and townsmen rushed to join the crusade, both from Hungary and from neighboring countries.

Turkish ships had blockaded Belgrade to prevent relief forces from reaching it. With his fleet strategically disposed, his cannons trained on the city's walls, and his army — as many as 150,000 strong — encamped before the target, Mehemmed was understandably complacent. After all, he had just taken the most impregnable city in Christendom; Belgrade should be a walkover. It was June of 1456. The bombardment was to begin in July, and the Turks were meanwhile raiding the surrounding country. Once the shelling of the city began, it would go on for two weeks. Before it started in earnest, however, the first crusading army was still able to break through the line of ships that attempted to bar their way, and enter the city to the sound of music.

When it became clear that the Turks were about to cut the city off more completely from all outside contact, St. John slipped out of Belgrade, promising to return with an army that would astonish both Turks and Christians. Meanwhile, the defenders were appalled at the sheer number of men and especially of artillery mustered by the Turks, which Hunyadi said was four times as much as the Turks had ever previously assembled. The bombardment was in full swing by the time St. John returned. When Hunyadi saw the motley crowd that the priest was bringing him, he declared he could not fight with such an untrained force. According to some reports, he had begun to think that

a truce with the sultan was the only way to save at least some
lives in this terrible extremity. The saint disagreed, arguing ve-
hemently and promising victory, and the hero at last yielded to
his friend's entreaties.

The whole story of the siege and of the inspired tactics of the
defenders, both on land and water, is too much to tell in detail
here. During the battles, Capistrano would stand on a high
point of the shore, within sight of both Turks and Christians,
waving a banner of the cross and calling out the name of Jesus.
He spent much time at an inland camp receiving each group of
new volunteers as it came in and knelt for his blessing. He also
evacuated the sick and wounded from the fortress to upstream
villages. He hardly ate or slept, though food was plentiful, for
now crusaders were coming from Germany, Poland, Bohemia,
and elsewhere — thousands of them. They were not professional
soldiers but they venerated St. John so highly that they would
follow him anywhere. Priests and religious came with the new
contingents, celebrating Mass, chanting their office, and hearing
confessions. One soldier is said to have remarked, "We have a
holy captain. We must avoid all sin." The battle cry St. John gave
them was "Jesus, Jesus, Jesus!"

The one weak point in the Turkish forces was soon revealed,
and as usual it was their seamanship. Particularly in the case of
Belgrade, a fortress-city situated at the confluence of two rivers,
naval strategy was essential to blockading and bombarding it.
The Turkish vessels were clumsy, their sailors inexperienced, and
the Hungarian ships had little trouble with them. Still, in the
last two days of the battle, hope alternated with despair, as the
Turks broke into the city and some defenders began to escape,
fearing all was lost. The tide turned again, however, and when
the Christians finally repelled the Turks' offensive, it appeared
that the battle was won. The remnants of the Turkish army were

still large enough to make the defenders wary, and it was forbidden to attack them in case they were laying ambushes instead of preparing to retreat.

Then it was that a small group of crusaders began firing on some Turks, who fled, and a large number of other Christians began to leave cover and attack, disobeying orders. St. John attempted to call them back, but his voice went unheard. He went outside the walls to bring them back, but when defenders inside the fortress saw him, they rushed out to join him. Seeing such a throng approaching, the Turks began to flee and the Christians rushed forward, capturing the Turkish siege guns without a fight. St. John began to see God's will in this spontaneous attack, and shaking off those who would have restrained him, he followed the crowd and climbed onto a heap of dirt with his standard-bearer next to him. There he cheered the Christians on as they battled the Turkish reserves, waving his cross and shouting prayers. The sultan himself, furious and incredulous, charged into the battle and managed to cut off the head of one crusader before receiving an arrow in his thigh and being forced into ignominious retreat. He cursed the panicky flight of the Janissaries so fiercely that their leader turned back into the fray and was cut down before the sultan's eyes. At dusk, the crusaders returned to the fortress; the Turks had withdrawn to their camp, anxious to leave the place as soon as possible; they had lost about 50,000 men, 300 guns, and 27 boats. Belgrade was saved.

Now was the time, thought Hunyadi, to drive the Turks completely out of Europe. In a letter to the pope, he argued that it could be done "if Christendom were to rise." But Christendom did not rise, and Hunyadi himself died of a plague that struck the region a few days after the battle. St. John did not long survive him. He too fell ill, and by the end of October he was

dead. In December, the Serb leader George Brankovic, who had
fought at Varna, also died. Of the great Christian crusaders who
had battled the enemy for the last decades, only Skanderbeg
was left — but Skanderbeg was by no means finished with the
Turks.

MAIN WORKS CONSULTED

All the works cited in the previous chapter, as well as the
following:

Held, Joseph. *Hunyadi: Legend and Reality.*

Hofer, John, Rev. *St. John Capistran, Reformer.*

[Ducas quotation translated by Speros Vryonis, Jr., quoted in
Bostom, *The Legacy of Jihad.*]

Vryonis, Speros, Jr. *The Decline of Medieval Hellenism in Asia
Minor.* Quotation from the Ottoman historian is found on
p. 357.

Four

The Suffering of the Balkans

The fall of Constantinople freed Mehemmed's army for his great onslaught on the states of the Balkan Peninsula. The sultan's targets included the parts of Greece he not did already control, Serbia, Albania, Croatia, Bosnia, miscellaneous mini-states, and Venetian holdings. As we will see, he and his successors were able to bring them all under their sway. As for Hungary, the fall of Byzantium had made it the one surviving great power with interests and influence in the Balkans. Hungary's hegemony in the northern Balkan region, as well as its habit of supporting resistance to Turkish rule, made it an obstacle to Ottoman European expansion. Mehemmed had his eye on Hungary too. We will here follow his conquests of four of the Balkan areas: mainland Greece, Serbia, Bosnia, and Croatia.

The Campaign Unfolds

Under Mehemmed's father, Murad II, within the Ottoman government two parties had emerged: one favored Murad's own policy, which was to negotiate with areas he wished to control, with the aim of turning them into self-governing vassals that acknowledged him as their overlord. He preferred doing this peacefully rather than by war, and even a Byzantine historian credited him with concern and sympathy for the common people, whether or not they were Muslim. Murad's vizier, Hahl Djandarh, was called sneeringly by his opponents "companion of the infidel" because he supported Murad's policy; Djandarh and other like-minded advisors were interested in economic development and prosperity, which they thought were better served by peace than by war. They favored a sort of carrot-and-stick jihad over the scorched-earth-and-mass-murder variety.

On the other side was a militant group of advisors who advocated the traditional jihad by armed conquest instead of negotiated submission, and who blamed Murad for being too easy on the *dhimmi*, contrary to the teachings of Islam. With Mehemmed II, this jihad party triumphed. He had the unfortunate Hahl Djandarh, who had dissuaded him from an earlier attack on Constantinople, executed soon after his conquest of the city. After that, the proponents of violent jihad, with the sultan himself as the most zealous of them, had it all their own way; any moderation there had been at the Ottoman court had evaporated. From then on, the generally self-governing areas formerly ruled by vassals became Ottoman provinces, under direct Turkish rule, and aggressive war was the order of the day.

The Fate of Greece

Following the capture of Constantinople by the Fourth Crusade in 1204, much of the west of Greece had been carved up into principalities ruled by Western Europeans. With the restoration of the Byzantine Empire later in the thirteenth century, the emperor's rule had been reasserted over many of these areas, though some still remained under the control of Venetians or other Westerners. The Ottomans had targeted Greece from the time they had first crossed into Europe in the mid-fourteenth century and, as mentioned earlier, they had captured the northern area around the city of Thessalonica and deported many of its citizens, as well as making other Greek conquests.

Now that the conquest of Constantinople had destroyed Byzantine rule for good, Mehemmed determined to smash any remaining Greek illusions about restoring — or at least holding onto — any part of the former Eastern Empire. Units of his army had been fighting Greek and Latin resistance in parts of Greece for decades, aided by the usual infighting among political rivals within the kaleidoscope of Greek despotates, principalities, and dukedoms. In 1446, an Ottoman force attacked the northwest part of the Morea, while another pushed south. The devastation was cruel: sources speak of sixty thousand people enslaved, in addition to the large numbers massacred, looted and ruined cities, and ravaged land.

A Tale of Two Brothers

One of the rulers of the area, who had been forced to make peace with the Turks under the usual harsh conditions, was Constantine IX, the heir of Byzantine emperor John VIII. When John died in 1448 and the ill-fated Constantine left Greece to assume his throne — only to die fighting the Turkish invaders five years later, as we have seen — he had left two sons in charge of his Peloponnesian territories. One, Thomas, supported the Union of Florence and reconciliation with Catholicism; the other, Demetrius, who was not above dealing with the Turks for his own purposes, opposed the Union.

The brothers began to quarrel, with each other and with the neighboring Venetian cities with which they should have been making common cause against the Turks. Meanwhile the Ottoman army busied itself during the 1450s with taking over other Greek territories that had so far escaped them. Just before taking Constantinople, Mehemmed had attacked the Morea again to make sure there would no question of support from Greece for the beleaguered city. Now, in possession of the Byzantine capital, he was ready to mop up all leftover Greek opposition. He actually received several invitations to intervene in the Morea and this is how it happened.

In 1453, the year of the great siege of Constantinople, two revolts broke out against the rule of Thomas and Demetrius. One began as a rebellion of Albanians who had been migrating into the Morea for some time, and resented an increase in their taxes; while some of these rebels attacked Demetrius, another group led by an adventurer with political ambitions moved against Thomas. Both groups appealed for help to the Turks. Meanwhile each of the brothers had taken refuge in one of his remaining fortresses, from which — incredible as it sounds — they also appealed to Mehemmed for assistance. The sultan must have rubbed his hands in glee; rarely had he been urged by so many of his victims to come and visit. He certainly was not about to encourage the rebel Albanian pretensions, with their compatriot, the formidable Skanderbeg, still going strong to the north; he therefore sent his army to the party with other intentions.

In December 1453 the Ottoman force arrived and suppressed both rebellions during the following months. The two brothers were reinstated but saddled with a heavy tribute; Mehemmed also placed some of their former lands under his direct control.

Thus the rulers' tax base was reduced, and soon they were years behind in their payments to the Turks. Typically, Demetrius tried to cope with an increasingly impossible situation by currying favor with the sultan, while Thomas, the Catholic, tried to get help from the West. In 1458 the Turks returned, confiscating even more of the brothers' land and raising the tribute even higher; they were harder on the lands of the less compliant Thomas than on the groveling Demetrius, but the results were much the same for both.

True to form, Demetrius accepted the settlement, which included the installation of an Ottoman governor in Corinth, while Thomas led the few Western mercenaries he had managed to hire in a failed attempt to recover one of his cities. He also captured some of Demetrius' forts, possibly out of resentment at his collaboration and the somewhat better position it had earned for him. This internecine strife continued for some years, exacerbated by plundering bands of Albanians who saw an opportunity for themselves. Mehemmed was occupied with other campaigns and did not immediately give his full attention to the Greek situation.

The End of the Tale

Then in 1459, Pope Pius II called for a new crusade, and the sultan decided he had better secure Greece before he had to fight another Western army. In early 1460 he entered the country in person with a large army, massacring the entire populations of some cities, and by the end of the year he was in possession of all but two strongholds. One fell the following year, and the other was ceded to the Turks by Venice some years later. Thomas fled to Italy where he was given a papal pension for the rest of his life. Demetrius was at first rewarded by the Turks with lands and position in Thrace, before falling out of favor and dying in a monastery.

Mehemmed had initially demanded Demetrius' daughter Helen for his harem, but then changed his mind, apparently out of fear — based on what evidence we do not know — that she would poison him. (She must have been a formidable character, to scare somebody like Mehemmed.) In retaliation, he forbade her to marry anybody else, and so she died unwed. Her death was apparently from natural causes, though one wonders. It was never good for one's health to scare somebody like Mehemmed.

One by one the various regions and towns of Greece, both north and south, were taken over by Mehemmed, with large numbers of inhabitants deported to other areas of his empire. The Venetians put up a fight for some of the towns they controlled, and held onto a couple of them until well into the following century, but in the end all became Ottoman. In Athens the Parthenon, which had long been the Church of Our Lady, became a mosque like many other Christian places of worship. There were, however, the numerous isles of Greece that remained unconquered, which we will explore later on.

Pope Pius II: The Lonely Crusader

Long before his election as Pope Pius II in 1458, the humanist scholar Aeneas Sylvius had realized the grave peril in which Europe stood as the Turks turned west on their way to conquer the world for Allah. He had repeatedly urged concerted action to defend the helpless states in the way of the marauders, but his words had fallen into the void. Now in 1458, shortly after his election, he began again to preach the crusade and called for a congress to be held at Mantua the following year to organize it. He opened the Congress of Mantua on June 1, but to his great frustration and disappointment, none of the invited heads of the major European powers had come, and even those rulers who sent representatives did not authorize them to make any arrangements on their behalf. The Holy Roman Emperor pleaded other urgent business; of the many German princes and dukes, a few eventually showed up, but mostly to pursue their own agendas with other members of the Congress. Not even all the Italian states were represented, at a time when the Turks were moving toward the Balkan coasts opposite Italy.

On the other hand, the Congress was well attended by desperate messengers from the states under attack, pleading for help: from Greece, Bosnia, and elsewhere they brought to the Congress eyewitness reports, which seem to have moved few except Pius and his small number of supporters. Even some of the cardinals began to criticize the pope openly. At news of the fall of Smederevo, in Serbia, the realistic pope remarked, "Now there is nothing to keep the Turks from attacking Hungary." Pius waited nearly three months in Mantua, hoping for a change of heart in the absent rulers. Eventually a number of key Italian states sent delegates, including even reluctant Venice. Of prominent rulers, though, only King Matyas of Hungary and Skanderbeg of Albania were firmly committed.

In his address to the Congress, the pope described the atrocities and sacrileges that had accompanied the Turkish conquest of Constantinople, strongly urged a united Christian response against a danger that threatened what was left of Christendom, and laid out the feasibility of such an enterprise.

People say . . . that now we shall have peace; but can we expect peace from a nation which thirsts for our blood, which has
already planted itself in Hungary [i.e., its southern border ar-
eas] after having subjugated Greece? Lay aside these infatuated
hopes. Mahomet will never lay down his arms until he is either
wholly victorious or completely vanquished. Each success will be
only a stepping-stone to the next until he has mastered all the
Western Monarchs, overthrown the Christian Faith, and imposed
the law of his false prophet on the whole world. . . . Oh, that
Godfrey, Baldwin, Eustace, Hugh, Boemund, Tancred, and those
other brave men who re-conquered Jerusalem were here! Truly
they would not need so many words to persuade them. They
would stand up and shout as they did of old before Our predecessor Urban II: 'God wills it! God wills it!' You wait in silence
and unmoved for the end of our discourse. . . .

The last words reveal the cynical mood of the assembly, of which
the pope was well aware.

Other meetings followed the close of the Congress in January
1460, and priests and monks were sent throughout Europe to
preach the crusade; large audiences heard them with enthusiasm,
and many volunteers took the Cross. They were not rulers or
military leaders, however, but ordinary men; the great ones of
Christendom hung back. Still, both the Congress and the subsequent consultations caused Mehemmed some concern. With
one eye on the progress of the plans for the crusade, he avoided
getting too involved in some of his projects. He need not have
worried. The crusade was scheduled to depart in 1464, and
in 1462 Pope Pius, despite his chronic ill health, announced
his intention of leading the expedition in person, as Pope St.
Gregory VII had dreamed of doing. The Bull of the Crusade,
issued in September 1463, was an eloquent exhortation to the
Christians of Europe to act — if not out of charity and devotion
to the Faith, at least out of self-interest:

> Take pity on your brethren, or, in any case, take pity on your-
> selves; for the like fate is hanging over you, and if you will not
> assist those who live between you and the enemy, those who live
> further away will forsake you also when your turn comes. . . .
> The ruin of the emperors of Constantinople and Trebizond, of
> the kings of Bosnia and Rascia, and other princes who have been
> overpowered, one after another, proves how disastrous it is to
> stand still and do nothing. As soon as Mahomet has subdued the
> East, he will quickly master the West.

In a bitter address to the Cardinals, he castigated them for
their lack of support and objections to his efforts, and blamed
the lack of zeal of the clergy:

> On every single thing we do, the people put the worst interpre-
> tation . . . the priesthood is an object of scorn . . . and, if we
> are willing to tell the truth, the luxury and pride of our Curia
> is excessive. This makes us so hateful to the people that we are
> not listened to even when we tell the truth. What do you think
> we ought to do in such circumstances? . . . We must change to
> paths long disused. We must ask by what means our elders won
> for us this far-flung rule of the Church and employ those. . . .
> Abstinence, purity, innocence, zeal for the Faith, religious fervor,
> scorn of death, eagerness for martyrdom. . . .

"Paths long disused." What an indictment of the Renaissance
clergy.

Nothing would dissuade the pope from leading the Crusade.
In May of 1464 he duly left Rome, saying he would never see it
again, for Ancona, the meeting point for ships and men. There
were pitifully few crusaders in Ancona, almost none of them
disciplined professional soldiers, and only a few ships. With
no arms or provisions, the men began to disperse; although a
few Venetian ships subsequently arrived, it was clear that no
Crusade would take place. Pope Pius saw the ruin of his great
plan for the saving of Christendom even as he himself was dying.

On August 14 he addressed the faithful cardinals around his deathbed for the last time, and on the following day — the Feast of the Assumption — he expired. The crusade died with him, to Mehemmed's relief. Now he could get on with his Balkan business and do it thoroughly this time.

Brankovic and Son Leave Serbia Vulnerable

Of the whole jigsaw puzzle of states, principalities, and mini-enclaves that made up the Balkan Peninsula, Serbia had long been the most powerful. In the previous century, under the great King Stephen Dušan (one of the few who seem to have realized the magnitude of the Ottoman threat), Serbia had developed a Balkan empire that rivaled Byzantine power in the region. Then came the disastrous Battle of Kosovo in 1389, discussed in chapter three; Serbian power was seriously reduced, and fifteenth-century rulers were still preoccupied with reconstructing it.

George Brankovic, who ruled Serbia from 1427 to 1456, had spent most of his reign scheming to expand his territory at the expense of his neighbors, or quarreling with Venice and with Hungary. He had been satisfied with the peace settlement he had made with the Turks in 1443, at the time of the Crusade of Varna, and subsequently declined to support any projected anti-Ottoman campaigns. This policy did not buy him much time, however; when he died at an advanced age in 1456, Serbia had only three years of independent national existence left.

During the last years of his life, Serbian history was a bewildering series of military campaigns against a variety of enemies (none of them Turks) with the goal of expanding Serbian territory. In 1453, Serbs were required by the Ottomans to support the assault on Constantinople. They were rewarded for this the following year . . . when the Turkish army began to raid their country. In 1455, a major Ottoman assault began against Serbia, which left Brankovic with a greatly reduced territory. Large numbers of captives were taken back to Ottoman Constantinople as part of the Turkish effort to repopulate the devastated and largely abandoned city.

In 1456, as we also saw in chapter three, the Turks were occupied with the siege of Belgrade, but they plundered Serbia as a matter of course when they passed through it both coming and going; it must have broken the heart of the old ruler, by now in his eighties, but he wasn't quite finished yet. Though one mention of his death on Christmas Eve of 1456 attributes it to grief and illness, other sources recount a less passive end. They claim he was ambushed by one of his many enemies (a Hungarian,) wounded in the fight — one cannot imagine him not defending himself — and held for ransom. Like the Byzantine emperor John V, whom we met in chapter two, the Serb ruler found that his son Lazar was most unwilling to part with the large ransom in gold demanded by his father's captors. Lazar does not seem to have been fond of either of his parents, but finally his mother's pleas wore him down and he forked over the money — though with an ill grace. His father's wound — the loss of two fingers — became infected, and finally killed him. No matter what the physical cause of death, it must have been made more bitter for the old warrior as he saw his beloved Serbia on the brink of extinction.

It would be disagreeable to have to report that the very undutiful Lazar succeeded his father, which he did, were it not for what happened to him some thirteen months later. On his accession, he seems to have immediately plunged into strife with his own family, nagging his mother mercilessly about his inheritance (some say actually having her poisoned) and wrangling with other relatives who claimed the throne. He also attacked the lands of some of the Hungarians involved in the obscure quarrel that had led to his father's death; this precluded his asking for Hungarian help as the Turks closed in. Whether of poison, natural illness, or terminal nastiness, Lazar himself died on January 20, 1458.

The Death of Serbian Independence

Within the next three months — until the arrival of the Turks in force — emergence of a new government was delayed by family quarrels as well as by the division between those who favored seeking aid from Hungary and those who advocated submission to and cooperation with the Ottomans. Both factions intrigued with both sides, Hungary and the Turks. When Hungary sent eight thousand troops to the Danube frontier (a move applauded by Helen, Lazar's widow), Michael Angelovic, a former government minister vying for power, requested Turkish troops to supplement his own in Smederevo, naively thinking of them as allies. When they arrived and raised the Turkish flag, the townspeople revolted, killing many Turks, and imprisoning Michael. Unfortunately, the Hungarian force was not large enough to intervene when an Ottoman army led by Michael's own brother, who had converted to Islam, entered Serbia in the spring of 1458.

It took a year for the Ottomans to gain control of the various regions of Serbia, because Mehemmed had other campaigns going at the same time and knew he could take his time with the helpless Serbs. During that year, factions and would-be rulers continued both to squabble among themselves and to seek outside help. The new king of Hungary, Hunyadi's son Matyas Corvinus, was too hard pressed both to consolidate his own position within his country and to provide for defense of its borders against the Turks, to do much for the Balkans. Helen then sought help from Bosnia by means of a marriage alliance of her daughter and the Bosnian ruler's heir. Once that was settled, Bosnia agreed to accept the suzerainty of Hungary, in the hope of gaining Hungarian protection.

Ironically, almost all that remained of free Serbia was the fortress-town of Smederevo, which had earlier revolted against the arrival of Turkish troops, so it was there that the royal wedding was celebrated in April 1459 and a new regime was set up. Naturally the Ottomans then moved in, and in June they took the town. Although Hungary was able to recover part of Serbia seventeen years later, it was only temporarily, since Hungary itself was soon to fall. Serbia itself would not again emerge as a free state for four hundred years.

Discord in Bosnia

Like other Balkan states, Bosnia was often wracked by political turmoil over succession to the throne. In the 1440s, turmoil became outright civil war, which prevented either side from responding in force to the papacy's plea for support for the Crusade of Varna in 1443. And the Turks were always quick to take advantage of the existence of rival political candidates, supporting whichever one suited their purposes.

The rightful ruler was the King Stefan Tomas, who ruled from 1443 to 1461. He was a convert to Catholicism, apparently from the "Bosnian Church." This somewhat obscure entity has often been identified with the Bogomil or Manichean heresy, a dualistic cult something like that of the Cathars in France, which flourished in the medieval Balkans. It seems, however, to have been

actually distinct from that sect and been centered around Bosnian
monks who considered themselves Catholic but somehow independent from the universal Church. The "Bosnian Church" had
probably emerged in the 1200s, but only began to attract Catholic attention in the following century. The papacy naturally
worked to reconcile these separatists, usually with the help of
Dominican missionaries and pressure from Catholic Hungary,
which traditionally controlled the northern part of Bosnia. All
this seems to have intensified the animosity already felt for Hungary by Bosnians, whether heretics, "Bosnian Church" members,
Orthodox, or even Catholics, for political reasons. Still, Bosnia
as a whole had long been a Catholic country, with permission to
use a Slavic liturgy.

At the time of King Stefan's reign, there were many conversions
to Catholicism in Bosnia, many churches were being built, and
Western Catholic culture was flourishing. The Ottoman threat
had reminded Bosnians of the need for Western support, and
the Faith was a strong link between their country and the West.
During the 1430s, even as the Turkish menace grew, Franciscan
missionaries were working in Bosnia under their holy Vicar, St.
James of the March, who did not find them easy to deal with.
Many of them were not living in monasteries (there were few
monasteries at the time in Bosnia) as St. James had ordered them
to do. The king took the side of the Franciscans in their practice
of living with families in order to reach people in areas where
there were no monasteries. Such discord between St. James, the
king, and the monks continued for some time as the Vicar strove
to reform discipline and fight heresy.

St. James was used to dealing with tricky situations. He was
a lawyer who had been at the Council of Florence, trying to reconcile the Greeks to Rome, and at the Council of Basle, working
for the return of the Hussite heretics to the Church. He was

sent on missions to many countries, including Hungary, as the successor to St. John Capistrano. He preached crusades against the Turks, worked numerous miracles, converted many souls, and would die at the age of eighty-five in Naples. During his time in Bosnia, however, not even he could remedy the problems caused by too few priests and monks and, for several reasons including Orthodox opposition, a lack of Catholic territorial organization within the country.

Too many Bosnians never saw a priest and did not have a parish church. Despite the real progress made in the 1430s under King Stefan, there was not enough time left for even saints to overcome the indifference of many Bosnians to religion. This apathy was partly the result of their lack of contact with the Church, as well as the bad example given by many nobles who had a habit of switching religions with ease. The coexistence of many quarreling religious groups within the country also tended to breed cynicism about any one of them being the true Church. Accordingly, after the Turkish conquest the Bosnians would be among the most willing recruits to Islam, and the country has the dubious distinction of being one of only two Balkan territories where large-scale conversions to the religion of the Muslim conquerors occurred.

A Tale of Two Stefans

The main rival of King Stefan of Bosnia in the 1440s and 1450s was one Stefan Vukcic, who was supported by the Turks and, because of family connections, by the Serbian king and Turkish vassal whom we have already met, George Brankovic. The civil war that resulted was finally settled temporarily with a truce, but since it was to the Turks' interest to stir up division with the country, we soon find Stefan Vukcic declaring that the territory he ruled was now independent from Bosnia. He continued to make trouble, supporting the Serbs against the Bosnians in a territorial war and also continuing to fight his own king. And all the while the Turks were methodically nibbling away at Bosnia from the east. Both the king and the renegade prince were forced to pay tribute, and the sums increased as the sultan needed more money from his victims to pay for his conquest of them.

Papal diplomacy smoothed over new friction between the king and Vukcic, but revolts within the country and hostilities with neighboring states continued to mark King Stefan's reign as he struggled to pay the massive Turkish tribute. In 1456, the Ottomans demanded the surrender of some major Bosnian towns. When the king refused, raids on his country were stepped up. After Serbia fell, Stefan appealed to the papacy for help and was told he needed to take action against the Bosnian Church, which he did: he gave the sect's clergy the choice of conversion or leaving the country, and most converted. Yet no assistance came from the West.

When King Stefan died in 1461, his son sent ambassadors to Pope Pius II, to request the papal crown his father had not dared to accept for fear of Turkish retaliation, and asked for bishops to help better organize the Church within Bosnia. The ambassadors also brought ominous news: the king had learned that the Ottoman invasion of Bosnia was planned for the summer of 1462. In a long letter included by Pope Pius II in his diary, King Stefan also wrote that the Turks were promising Bosnian peasants that they would be free and well treated by the Turks. The peasants already knew that peasants in neighboring conquered territories paid much lower taxes; the high taxes in Bosnia were due to the need to prepare for war and

pay the crushingly high Turkish tribute, but the peasants did
not think of that. After warning that after Bosnia the Turks
would next move against Croatia, Dalmatia, Hungary, Venice,
and Rome itself, the king added, "My father predicted to your
predecessor and the Venetians the fall of Constantinople. He
was not believed. . . . Now I prophesy about myself. If you trust
and aid me I shall be saved; if not, I shall perish and many will
be ruined with me."

The pope urged the king to contact the king of Hungary,
Matyas Corvinus, and sent papal envoys to Hungary and Venice.
In 1462, as King Stefan had predicted, the beginning of the end
came. Several events precipitated it. For one thing, the Turks were
well aware of King Stefan's embassy to the pope, his contacts
with Hungary, and — probably — his receipt of the apostolic
crown. Pope Pius mentions also that King Stefan had refused to
make his tribute payment to the Turks.

Then the son of his father's old antagonist, Stefan Vukcic, now
calling himself *Herceg*, ("Duke") from which comes the name of
his territory Hercegovina, revolted against his father and asked
the Turks to send help. By 1463 the massive Ottoman assault
was underway, at first camouflaged as an expedition against
Hungary before it was redirected at a strategic moment. The
king fled to a fortress that he was persuaded to surrender in
exchange for his freedom; once he had surrendered, however, he
was taken prisoner. Again, to save his life, he complied with an
order to surrender all of Bosnia's fortresses, after which he was
beheaded. His written orders were then sent to all the fortresses,
and the commanders obeyed the king's orders. A vast sum of
money also fell into the Turks' hands.

The speed with which all this happened — the country was
under Turkish control within weeks — is partially explained by
the surprise attack, and the orders of surrender extracted from

the king. More nebulous are the reasons for the demoralization attributed by some historians to the Bosnians at this period. They must have been aware for some time that they were doomed, but some thought the Turks would get them and some thought the Hungarians would, possibly as part of a war against the Turks. They did not like either alternative, but many were said to have preferred the Turks. At least, a desperate delegation that went to Venice after Bosnia's fall apparently made the point that they would not mind if Venice took over the country, but if it would not do so, they would prefer to stay under Turkish rule — anything rather than be ruled by their hereditary enemies. "Better the Turks than the Hungarians" — an eerie echo of "better the turban than the tiara" — expresses a point of view that is not easy to understand, knowing what we do about the Turks.

Dracula and the Fall of Wallachia

Meanwhile, Serbia's neighbor, Wallachia, also fell under Turkish control. This territory, of changing boundaries and confusing history, lay east of Serbia, north of Bulgaria, and south of the Hungarian region of Transylvania. It would become, much later, the heart of modern Rumania. Like the other Balkan states, it suffered from internal political rivalries and friction with neighboring Moldavia, which it periodically tried to conquer. Wallachia had been a very early Ottoman target when the Turks first moved against Bulgaria in the fourteenth century. Its Vlach population had succeeded in defeating a number of Turkish attacks, and one of its kings had later fought with the Serbs against the Turks at Kosovo. Another ruler, Vlad II Dracul, had been the valuable ally of King Sigismund of Hungary in the early fifteenth century. By 1456 when his son — Vlad the Impaler, the historical model for the fictional Dracula — came to the throne (for the second time; he had reigned briefly earlier) with the support of Janos Hunyadi, Wallachia was under Turkish suzerainty.

Vlad refused to allow the Turks to collect the *devşirme*, and Mehemmed sent in two thousand men to enforce it and seize Vlad, who proceeded to impale them all and take the offensive into Turkish territory. The ferocious sultan himself then led a large army against Vlad in 1462. As Skanderbeg had done, Vlad withdrew into his dense forestlands where the Ottoman army could not follow. Once he was said to have penetrated the Turkish camp at night in disguise, in an attempt to assassinate the sultan, but failed to find the right tent. Apparently he managed to repel the Turkish advance, and was only defeated when a rival prince from Moldavia attacked part of his forces at the same time as the Turks attacked the other part.

Temporarily beaten, he fled to Hungary while the Turks set his younger brother, a convert to Islam, on the throne. Hungary, however, had recognized his turncoat brother, the new puppet ruler of Wallachia, and proceeded to detain Vlad for some time, during which he became a Catholic. How long he stayed in Hungary and what he did for the next several years is unclear and some of it seems very unpleasant, so we can skip to 1476 when Vlad surfaced and again regained his throne with foreign help. As the Ottoman army once more approached with a replacement candidate, Vlad found that he had little support among either the upper or lower classes of his country. He does not seem to have been at all a nice man, and if only some of the rumors of his cruelties to his people are true, it is no wonder he was nearly abandoned in the end.

When the next confrontation with the Ottomans came, probably in late 1476, Vlad either: a) defeated them and was then killed by one of his own men, or b) was defeated and killed by the Turks; or c) was killed by domestic enemies at some other time. However you look at it he certainly died, though his place of burial is as much a mystery as the details of his demise. In any case Wallachia, like the rest of the Balkans, was now definitively part of Mehemmed's empire.

Moldavia Resists

Wallachia's hostile neighbor, Moldavia, would fall too, though it had its brief moment of glory. In the late 1450s, Stephen the Great came to the throne and proceeded to attack now-Turkish Wallachia and replace the Turks' puppet on the throne with his own candidate. This occurred while Mehemmed was busy in Asia Minor with Karamania, so Stephen had the time to communicate with the papacy, Venice, Uzun Hasan in Persia, and various European states in order to assemble allies. By the time Mehemmed got around to sending an army into Moldavia, Stephen had troops from both Poland and Hungary fighting alongside his own. He achieved a great victory at Racova over the Turks in 1475, as Hunyadi, Skanderbeg, and Vlad had done. By the following year, however, Mehemmed had conquered an area of the Black Sea coast where Tartars lived, and requisitioned them for his campaign of revenge against Moldavia.

This time, as Mehemmed marched toward the country, Stephen no longer had foreign troops to help him as he found himself under attack from a prince he had himself placed on the throne of Wallachia. Assailed on one side by Wallachians and on the other by Tartars, he was unable to confront the Ottoman army effectively and was defeated after suffering heavy losses. He was not quite vanquished, however, and the sultan finally withdrew without having fully conquered the country. Eight years later, the Turks managed to conquer two key fortresses as Stephen pinned his hopes on an Eastern European alliance of Hungary, Poland, Lithuania, and Moscow, which failed to materialize. On his deathbed in 1504, he advised his son to submit to the Turks; there was no other hope of survival for his people. Moldavia had held out longer than most of Mehemmed's targets, but submission became its tragic fate too.

Catholic Croatia Is Plundered

This northern Balkan territory had traditionally been within Hungary's sphere of influence and under Hungarian suzerainty — the Hungarian kings' title was "King of Hungary and Croatia" — though with a ruler of its own called a Ban. It was Catholic, provided an outlet to the sea for Hungary, and was certainly vital to the defense of Central Europe against the Turks.

When Bosnia fell, the Turks began raiding Croatia, again taking thousands of prisoners. King Matyas of Hungary was too occupied with other international problems to come to Croatia's aid, so the Ban appealed to the Habsburgs and the Venetians. This triggered a military invasion by Matyas, who annexed some Croatian territory, appointed a new Ban, and antagonized the people with his heavy-handed actions. Even as the Ottoman raids intensified, various factions within Croatia, like all the factions within all the other Balkan states, were quarreling and intriguing for political advantage. Things had quieted down, and relations with Hungary partially smoothed over, by 1490, but then Matyas died. He had been a great king from many points of view and on hearing of his death the serfs and peasants lamented, "King Matyas is dead; justice has fled." A dispute over the succession to the throne — always a weak point in

Hungarian government — then developed, and by the time it was settled with Ulászló II as king, the Turks were mounting massive attacks on both Croatia and Slovenia.

The new king met them in 1493 with a combined Hungarian and Croatian army, which suffered a resounding defeat. Now parts of Croatia were paying tribute to the sultan; the Turkish raids at this time seem to have been for the purposes of plunder and captives rather than annexation. Until 1520, this nibbling away at the Croatian population and resources continued, punctuated by a few battles between Hungarian-Croatian forces and the Turks. The massive Turkish campaign against Hungary in 1526 would involve much of Croatia also, except for small pockets here and there and a portion that came under Habsburg control, as we will see later.

Meanwhile, Mehemmed had one of his most formidable opponents still to deal with: Albania.

Main Works Consulted

The New Cambridge Medieval History, vol. VII.

Carroll, Warren H. *A History of Christendom*, vol. III. Quotation p. 332.

Fine, John V. A., Jr. *The Late Medieval Balkans*. I am have relied extensively on this splendid survey for details of the Balkan situation, which was one of bewildering complexity. A few of the author's conclusions are debatable, but his lucid presentation of the facts is a Godsend for the non-specialist in Balkan history. King Stefan Tomasovic quotation p. 584.

Halecki, Oscar. *Borderlands of Western Civilization*.

Kinross, Lord. *The Ottoman Empire.*

Macartney, C. A. M. *Hungary.*

Pastor, Ludwig von. *History of the Popes*, vol. III. Quotation from the Bull of the Crusade p. 332.

Pius II, Pope. *Memoirs of a Renaissance Pope.* Quotation from the address to the Cardinals p. 357; from the address to the Congress of Mantua p. 80.

Five

Albania, Rhodes, Otranto

The sixth scene that unfolds in this drama of Ottoman conquest has several set changes. Mehemmed was busier than ever in the 1470s, sending armies all over Asia Minor, the Balkans, and the Mediterranean, and leading major campaigns in person. In many of those battles the Ottoman fleet was involved, a fleet that only twenty years after its unimpressive showing at the siege of Constantinople, now rivaled that of Venice. How did that happen?

It was Mehemmed II, again, who seems to have first realized the importance of developing a navy, not only for conquest (always what he liked best) but also for trade and transport. Before his time, the Ottomans had relied largely on Christian ships for transporting their troops into Europe from Asia, as well as for ferrying Turkish tribesmen assigned to colonize conquered Christian lands. The Italian mercantile republic of Genoa was only too willing to serve the Turks in this way. After the fall of Constantinople, however, Genoa's Black Sea routes were closed off, and the Republic disposed of its colonies and commercial interests in Asia Minor to a joint stock company and vanished from the scene. Their ships had given Mehemmed lots of ideas, though, about the kind of vessels he wanted in his own fleet, and he soon had a large number of copycat vessels built of various sizes and types. There were plenty of experienced men available to design, build and sail the ships from among the large number of Christian employees, renegades, adventurers, and captives who served the sultan, and finding the mass of slaves required to man the oars was no problem for a Turkish ruler.

The fleet gave Mehemmed's adventures a new dimension, and he sent it scooting all over the Aegean, Adriatic, and eastern Mediterranean seas on his business of war.

Albania Stymies the Sultan

In the Balkans, there remained Albania and the incomparable Skanderbeg. The Turks had long had it in for the renowned Albanian, but he had also become a great hero to Christians all over Europe. Thus when the Turks began to raid Albania in 1455, European volunteers from France, Germany and elsewhere, inspired by the already legendary exploits of the great ruler, fought at his side. The Ottoman raids were destructive and brutal, but their opponents paid them back: in one failed assault, the Turks lost over five thousand soldiers. Skanderbeg defeated another invasion in 1456, this one led by an Albanian renegade who afterward begged and received his pardon. It seems incredible that a national hero, leading his country in the struggle for its very existence, would have to suffer from traitors and renegades, but they turn up repeatedly in the saga of Skanderbeg; once even his own nephew joined the Turks.

In 1457, the Ottomans mounted a huge attack on the country with an army of perhaps sixty thousand. As usual in such a situation, the Albanian defenders retreated to the mountains, from which they could assault the enemy with guerilla tactics. The same year, the Albanians won another major battle and Mehemmed proposed an armistice. Skanderbeg refused, hoping

for the long-planned crusade Pope Pius II was trying to organize. The following year the indefatigable hero defeated another
Turkish attack, and because of its holdings on the Albanian
coast, Venice also was reluctantly drawn into the war against
the Turks.

There followed more or less of a stalemate until 1462; Skanderbeg even found time to go to Italy to help out an ally, the
King of Naples, in his war with a local enemy. In 1463, however,
the Ottomans sent in two invading forces that were to join up
inside the country. But Skanderbeg defeated the first of them,
preventing the juncture, and then rushed to meet and defeat the
other army. Now that he had the upper hand, he was at last
willing to make peace with Mehemmed, and signed the armistice
in 1463; evidently he had given up hope of the crusade and
wanted to negotiate under the most favorable circumstances,
before more Turks entered the country or his domestic support became eroded. He was also nearing sixty, and realized he
could not continue his rigorous life of almost constant warfare
indefinitely.

For reasons unknown, however, the truce was soon broken.
In 1464 another Turkish army was on the march into Albania,
this one led by yet another Albanian traitor. The destruction
caused by the Turks among the hapless population was such
that Skanderbeg had no mercy on the enemy when he defeated
them, killing even those who surrendered. The renegade was
back with another force the following year, and again they were
defeated. Meanwhile Skanderbeg was negotiating with Venice,
now the ally of Albania against the Turks.

Mehemmed was beside himself with fury at the spectacle of
little Albania repeatedly defeating the great Ottoman Empire. He
badly wanted the country's seacoast as a base from which to attack Italy, and so he was determined to see that things went right

in the next round. In 1466 he personally led an enormous force — as many as three hundred thousand men strong — against the city of Kroja. Skanderbeg again withdrew to the mountains with his army, leaving only a small garrison behind in the city. The sultan's army set in for a siege, while Skanderbeg proceeded to mount lightning hit-and-run attacks on the besiegers. Several weeks later, Mehemmed's considerably reduced army was still looking at the walls of Kroja from the outside. Humiliated, and no doubt even more furious, he gathered his remaining forces and went back to Constantinople. It seems however, that he left several garrisons in fortresses he had captured along the way, so there were now Turkish troops within Albania, and some areas that were outside Skanderbeg's control.

In December 1466, the Albanian hero was in Rome. An eyewitness described him as "an old man in his sixtieth year; he came with but few horses, in poverty; I hear that he will ask for help." The pope, now Paul II, received him with honors and friendship, and Skanderbeg left with a considerable sum of money from the pontiff and the cardinals, as well as funds from Venice and Naples. The ruler of Naples is said to have added arms and other supplies as well.

The following year Mehemmed returned, this time heading directly for the seacoast to try to take those ports he wanted. He besieged Durazzo and failed to take it; he besieged Kroja again and that failed too. Another offensive led by another Ottoman general was then defeated by Skanderbeg. Again Mehemmed withdrew, but again having won a small tactical victory: this time there were more Turkish forces in captured fortresses within Albania, and numerous citizens had been taken captive or had fled to Italy.

In January 1468, Albania and all of Europe were shaken by the news that Skanderbeg had died. (Mehemmed, on the other hand, is quoted as exulting: "At last Europe and Asia are mine. Woe to Christendom! She has lost her sword and her shield.") Yet even had Skanderbeg lived, he could not have resisted the relentless Ottoman assaults, nor could the country have long survived its depopulation, destruction, and loss of crops and livestock. The only thing that could have saved Albania was a great Western crusade, but even with the Turks just across the narrow Adriatic Sea, not even the Italian states were willing to answer the pope's frantic summons.

Once the hero was gone, the usual infighting broke out again among political factions within Albania. Skanderbeg's son, John, negotiated for more Venetian support, and he had the good fortune of a brief respite while the Turks were busy fighting Venice, particularly in its island possessions. They had also been forced into a campaign in Asia Minor to repress an enemy who had been cultivated by papal and Venetian diplomats. This was Uzun-Hasan, lord of Persia and much else, who controlled strategic trade routes and otherwise interfered with the Ottomans. Mehemmed subdued him temporarily in 1473, though only after suffering an initial defeat, which, as usual, infuriated him. After the subsequent victory, he is said to have taken three thousand prisoners whom he ordered executed at the rate of four hundred a day on his march back west. He also spent time in 1475 annihilating the emirate of Karamania that had long given him trouble. It was 1477 before the Turks again marched on Albania.

This time, after a yearlong siege, Kroja fell; the Turks killed all the males within the city and enslaved the women. Venetian towns fell, and the cathedral of Alessio became a mosque. The regions known as Zeta and Hercegovina were also conquered in the 1480s, but Skanderbeg's son John was not yet willing to surrender Albania. Mehemmed died in 1481, and John took advantage of the situation to mount a revolt that liberated much of Albania from its occupiers. The Ottomans sent in armies and again the Albanians defeated them. Western powers promised help to the resistance fighters, and the French king was trying to organize a crusade, but — could we expect anything else? — help never came. By this time the Ottomans were using their fleet and sent it up the Albanian coast, conquering town after town, although it took them far into the next century to take some of them.

Albania was Ottoman at last, but the Turks did not find it a very profitable acquisition. The terrain and the independence of the people made it difficult to govern; when mountainous areas refused to pay tribute there was no way to make them without spending more on campaigns than the tribute was worth. There was another factor in the lenient treatment doled out by the Turks. Many Albanians had embraced Islam, for some of the same reasons as the Bosnians. Lack of Christian institutions and clergy in the hinterland, especially in the north, had left the people vulnerable to Muslim proselytism. The sad result was that many of these tribal people who had once followed Skanderbeg later proved to be the most loyal supporters of the Turks and eager recruits for the Ottoman army. They even formed a special corps of bodyguards for the sultan. Skanderbeg's Catholic Albania was dead indeed.

Mehemmed's Next Move: Italy

Always fidgety without something or other to conquer, Mehemmed, in the last few years of his life, had begun striking on several fronts at once, busily sending out the now first-class Ottoman fleet as well as numerous raiding parties against Western targets. "But unless we put up strong resistance to the

Turks," Pope Pius had warned the cardinals in 1463, "it will not be long before both the Hungarians and the Venetians give way and then our liberty too is doomed." Mehemmed did not, however, wait to squash Venice and Hungary before heading for Italy. Turkish cavalry coming from northern Bosnia were already raiding northern Italy in 1477, looting towns and villages, and camping practically on the outskirts of Venice. Defeating the Venetians in battle, they left in the fall with their loot and a trail of devastation behind them. More would return in the spring — tens of thousands of them. These seem to have been irregular soldiers, and both their presence and their war cry of "Mehmed, Mehmed, Roma, Roma!" terrified the inhabitants. Venice was finally able to make peace with Mehemmed, on terms very advantageous to the Turks and onerous for Venice.

By 1480, Mehemmed felt free to land an army in the southern tip of Italy, from where he could move up the peninsula toward Rome, possibly with more raiders moving into the north from the Balkans again. He decided first, however, to send an army to take the island of Rhodes, very near the Turkish coast. He had been assured that this Christian blot on the Turkish landscape was ripe for the taking, and it would fill in the time until he was ready for the Italian expedition. This first Turkish siege of Rhodes lasted from May to August 1480, and is one of the most heroic episodes in the Christian anti-jihad.

The First Siege of Rhodes

The great fortress-island belonging to the Order of the Hospital of St. John of Jerusalem had been home to the Knights since they had been forced by Muslim victories to leave the Holy Land in 1291. They were soon admirably fulfilling their mission of fighting the infidel and assisting victims of Muslim attacks. When Orhan, son of Osman, the Ottoman founding father, had the idea of capturing a small Greek island and then attacking Rhodes, the Knights defeated the attack easily and went on to liberate the Greek island. From then on they were constantly called upon to help out victims of Ottoman aggression, from the Armenians to the Persian Uzun-Hasan, to whom they sent artillery experts and other advisors in his struggle against Mehemmed. Everywhere supporting the sultan's enemies while never themselves conquered, the Knights Hospitaller infuriated the Ottoman beyond measure. Their stronghold was even visible from the Turkish coast — a permanent symbol of the frustration of Turkish plans. How could the Ottomans take over the world if they could not even take over that Christian eyesore? So Mehemmed began methodically to plan his siege of the island in the late 1470s.

The Turks had raided Rhodes before, notably in 1457. Rhodes is a large island with several towns in addition to the great fortress-town of the Knights, and the raiding party was somehow able to land unopposed and damage crops, raze one of the larger towns, kill a number of the inhabitants, and take slaves before departing. The Knights took this as a punishment for the general deterioration of morality on the island, and the lack of discipline even within the Order. They took steps to restore both, beefed up their defenses, and were ready for the Turks when they came again, in 1469. With their families, crops, and animals moved within the walls of various castles, the Orthodox Rhodians were armed and lay in ambush together with the Catholic Knights. (No "better the turban than the tiara" here; the realists of Rhodes knew better.) The Turks landed, fell into the ambush, and suffered such damage that they soon withdrew. Mehemmed, impotently seething again, vowed repeatedly to take revenge on Rhodes during the next few years, but as we have seen he was distracted by several other problems.

The Knights knew he would keep his word, however, and in 1476 elected a Grand Master, Pierre d'Aubusson, well suited to the challenge. Mehemmed, on his side, had a number of Greek traitors who spied for him, and the leader of the expedition, Misac Pasha, was a descendent of the imperial Byzantine Palaeologus family; he had converted to Islam and now served the Turks. There was also a German engineer specializing in siege warfare who assured the sultan that the walls of Rhodes could not stand up to a modern artillery assault. This must have sounded plausible, since Mehemmed had already experienced what modern artillery could do, at the siege of Constantinople. The sultan sent an army into Rhodes on December 4, 1479 to test the reactions of the populace. Rhodes was ready for it and it withdrew.

The Knights' grand master, realizing a major attack was imminent, wrote to all the priors of the Order for support, as well as to the European powers. He set up the castle-shelters that would give refuge to the population, and had the precious icon of Our Lady of Graces moved from its monastery to the Cathedral of St. John. Soon it was April 1480, and Turkish forces were massed on the shore opposite Rhodes, while more were on ships approaching the island. The populace gathered on a hill to watch the spectacle, until the order was given for them to take shelter; homes and even churches outside the city were purposely destroyed and the rubble taken inside the fortress to prevent the Turks from using it.

The Turks landed on May 23, 1480, to the sound of the loud martial music they seem to have been the first to employ, and possibly to the wailing, shrieking cries of the dervishes inspiring the soldiers to heroism — a sound peculiarly unnerving to the ears of Western warriors. In the initial fighting one of the Knights was killed, along with one of the sultan's Greek spies. The Turks set up cannon to bombard the fort of St. Nicholas, which guarded the harbor, and the Knights responded with their own powerful guns. Then the German siege expert arrived unexpectedly at the gate of the Knights' main fortress of St. John and demanded entry; he'd had a change of heart, he said, and despite his twenty years of working for the Ottomans, he wanted now to place his talents at the service of the Knights. Pierre d'Aubusson hadn't been born yesterday, so he pretended to believe the man, allowing him to inspect the defenses (while being closely shadowed) from the inside. Before long he was safely in the fortress dungeon, having aroused suspicion (and having failed to deliver any useful advice). Before his execution, he confessed (under torture) to his deception, and warned that the Turkish army was 100,000 strong, including mine experts and that they had the most up-to-date siege equipment.

Within the fortress walls there were 250 Knights — some sources say 600, perhaps counting brethren who were not professed Knights — and some 2,500 armed civilians. There were also a number of mercenaries and men who just happened to be in Rhodes at the wrong time (one was the grand master's nephew, another a Hungarian on some business or other), bringing the total to about 3,500. There is also mention in the sources of one woman, Maria Archangelos, whom the grand master later praised, saying she had fought like the Amazons of old. The Turkish assailants, however, have been estimated to number 70,000; more — perhaps approaching the 100,000 warned of by the German siege expert — if you included the unpaid, undisciplined, and often vicious Bashi-Bazouks. These dregs of society from all over the Ottoman Empire generally made up the first lines of an Ottoman attack; they fought only for loot and were kept fighting by a police unit brandishing whips and clubs directly behind them.

On June 9 the Turks landed a large force at the fort of St. Nicholas. What happened next is not completely clear, but the

Turks were apparently beaten off (with perhaps 600 casualties) and withdrew. Meanwhile the Turkish cannon bombardment continued, and all through June and into July the huge stone balls continued to fall on the fortress of St. John, the sound carrying to islands sixty miles away. Families went underground to escape, but at night, through secret passages, men crept out to ambush as many Turks as possible.

The harbor fortress of St. Nicholas still had not fallen, so the Turks devised a new strategy: they made a pontoon bridge, attached a line to it, and ran the other end through a ring on an anchor they had attached to a rock beneath the fort. Thus they could haul on the rope from the beachhead where they had originally landed and pull the troop-laden platform to where the soldiers could jump off and attack the fort.

The plan was foiled, though, thanks to Roger Jervis, an English sailor who dived into the water and managed to cut the rope just in time. The platform and its troops floated out to sea under fire — both material and verbal — from the island.

The Turks, however, tried again, finally landing at the fort on June 18. The fighting that night was grim hand-to-hand combat, with Grand Master d'Aubusson first in line with his sword. When a stone knocked off his helmet, another Knight offered his. The Knights used the Byzantine invention "Greek fire" — a kind of incendiary liquid — to ignite the Turkish ships, and flames lit the battle as it raged all night. At dawn on June 19, the Turks withdrew from the area of the St. Nicholas fort. They had lost around 2,500 men in one night.

On the other side of the Knights' stronghold, outside the Italian quarter where the Turks had also been attacking, a greatly discouraged Misac Pasha shut himself up in his tent for three days before emerging to lead another offensive. The Turks dug trenches and attempted to sap the walls and fill in the great moat. From inside, the defenders showered the sappers with stones and clay pots filled with incendiary material. They dug their own tunnels and took away from below what the Turks were piling up from above, using it to build another line of walls. Arrows with messages began flying over the walls daily, offering peace to the Greeks of Rhodes if they would only allow the Turks to get at the Knights and destroy them. The Orthodox Greeks, however, remained loyal to the Christian cause. Misac Pasha tried sending two more phony deserters into the city, but they were caught in a plot to murder the grand master, and executed.

July 27 was the feast of St. Pantaleon, an early martyr venerated in both East and West, whose blood in a phial at Ravello liquefies on his feast day like that of St. Januarius. It was on that day that the Turks began their final assault on the Italian quarter, the attack that would surely take them inside the fortress-town. They even had their looting sacks ready, along with sharpened stakes. (It seems the plan was to kill every armed man in the town, enslave the women and children, and impale the Knights on the stakes.) Another bombardment of cannon balls began that morning, and the next day 2,500 Turks forced back the defenders and raised their flag on the tower of the Italian quarter. Then they began to descend the inside of the great walls into the town. Grand Master d'Aubusson led the defense, climbing to the tower of the Italian quarter to fight the Janissaries. He was wounded five times, (reminding his comrades of the five wounds of Christ), exhausted, and nearly sixty years old, yet he did not think of surrender but continued the fight, which went on for another couple of hours. Incredibly, the Turks began losing, and kept on doing so until they had been thoroughly defeated. One of d'Aubusson's wounds was to his lung which, given the medical deficiencies of the time, should have proved fatal. He survived, however, for another twenty-three years as grand master.

A Turkish version of this almost inexplicable reversal of fortune has it that word came to the troops that there was to be no looting, because everything in Rhodes was to belong to the sultan. The result of this report was that the troops outside the walls refused to advance and their comrades inside were slaughtered. Another theory for the puzzling defeat of the Turks is that the Bashi-Bazouks, crowded into near immobility by the press of the advance against the walls, and facing the formidable blows of the Knights, turned in blind panic and began to push to the rear despite the blows from the military police; this caused a chain reaction until the whole army was in flight.

A Christian chronicler of the siege, however, records a miraculous sign that appeared in the sky on that fateful morning and terrified the Turks into retreat: a golden cross with the Blessed Virgin and St. John, and behind them the Knights that had fallen in the battle. The Orthodox claimed the victory as a miracle for St. Pantaleon and built a new church for him next to the new Latin church of Our Lady of Victory.

It was not until August 17 that the Turks finally weighed anchor and left Rhodes harbor, having spent the intervening period ravaging the countryside and razing defenseless villages. Misac Pasha, poor apostate Greek, tried to take out his frustration on a Greek coastal town, but failed there too. When he got back to Constantinople the sultan, with amazing leniency — for him — punished him merely with exile.

Demolished and devastated Rhodes would be still more ruined when a series of earthquakes the following year toppled much of what had been left standing, including the St. Nicholas fort that had resisted all assaults of the Turks. But the death of Mehemmed would give the island a breathing space; years would pass before the Ottomans again came to Rhodes, but come they would.

Martyrdom in Otranto

The news from Rhodes having again unleashed his terrific temper, Mehemmed now sent an army to southern Italy in August 1480. He could do this with impunity, because the Venetian-Turkish treaty had neutralized the most powerful Italian fleet, that of Venice. (In any case, Venice was the rival of Naples, the chief power in the south and might not have been unhappy to see Neapolitan territory attacked.) Brindisi had been the original target, but Otranto was substituted because it seemed to the Turks an easier strategic target. The town was quickly taken in a surprise attack by cavalry, with much loss of life and many of the buildings burned. Of the some 22,000 inhabitants, 12,000 died, often hideously tortured in the Ottoman way, and most of the rest enslaved. Eight hundred who refused to convert to Islam were gruesomely put to death, their bodies thrown to dogs. They have since been beatified by the Catholic Church. The archbishop, taking his stand in front of the altar in his cathedral, remained praying with his priests around him and the Blessed Sacrament in his hands until the Turks took him and sawed him in two. The same hideous death — "the favorite Ottoman mode of intimidation," a historian has remarked — was meted out to the commandant.

The Turks ravaged the countryside, but their savagery proved counter-productive: they needed supplies for their move north to Rome, but curiously enough the surviving inhabitants could not be coaxed back to serve their enemy's needs. The Turks, in the course of their forays, began to face armed resistance from King Ferdinand of Naples. Ferdinand and Isabella of Spain sent troops and ships too, and soon the Turks were bottled up in Otranto. The sultan, however, was widely expected to arrive in person at any time.

In Rome, the panic was as keen as if Mehemmed were already at the gates. Pope Sixtus IV considered fleeing, but in the end decided to remain and send envoys throughout Italy and Europe to mobilize forces for the defense of the peninsula. He also sent Blessed Angelo Carletti de Chivasso, a Franciscan theologian, to preach a crusade against the Turks. Sixtus, like several other popes of his day, was embroiled in Italian affairs. As ruler of a central Italian state, he had intrigued and quarreled with the others, but now he urged a common front against the Turks and himself gave the example of making peace with his enemies. Meanwhile the siege dragged on, while defense funds were collected and more ships built. The king of England regretted that he couldn't possibly do anything to help; the German states could not agree on what, if anything, to do; France would help on condition that everybody else did too. The Italian states were more forthcoming, except for Venice, which was now allied with the Turks.

May brought surprising news of Mehemmed's death. The sultan had been in Asia in the spring; as usual, he had kept his plans secret, so it is not known whether he intended to besiege Rhodes again, invade Egypt, or do something else. Though he was only forty-nine, he had long been in poor health and it was partly his own fault. He ate and drank (despite his religion) to excess and grew fat, which worsened his arthritis and added gout, colic, and other obesity-related ills to his physical woes. Still, he had survived some fourteen Venetian attempts to poison him over the years, and almost seemed to lead a charmed life. One might have expected him to die of apoplexy, so prone does he seem to have been to irascibility and rage, but it was apparently something else that did him in.

In any case, his self-indulgent lifestyle caught up with him in May 1481. He developed severe colitis, and the medicine his doctor gave him did not help. Rumor had it that it was actually an overdose of opium ordered by his son and successor, but whatever it was it either hastened or at least did not forestall the end, which came on May 4. His death meant not just the lifting of the Muslim threat to Italy, where the Turkish garrison at Otranto obstinately held out until September before surrendering, but, as we shall see, forty years of freedom from any major Ottoman threat.

The death of Mehemmed and the subsequent withdrawal of the Ottoman army from Otranto was seen as God's answer to Blessed Angelo's mission, and it may well have been. Now the papacy and the other states of Western Europe could go back to their internecine struggles for riches and power. Only those Christians in the borderlands, such as Hungary, Rhodes, and the numerous and vulnerable islands, still scanned the horizon for the next approach of the Turkish armies or the Ottoman fleet.

MAIN WORKS CONSULTED

Bradford, Ernle. *The Shield and the Sword.*

Bury, J. B. "The Ottoman Empire," in *The Cambridge Modern History*, vol. I.

Fine, John V. A., Jr. *The Late Medieval Balkans.*

Pastor, Ludwig von. *History of the Popes*, vol. IV.

Pavlidis, Vangelis. *Rhodes 1306–1522.*

Seward, Desmond. *The Monks of War.*

Vryonis, Speros, Jr. *The Decline of Medieval Hellenism.*

Six

A Semi-Peaceful Interlude

This seventh scene in our drama is unexpectedly tranquil compared with its predecessors. The fighting among the European powers was going on as usual, but the combatants could concentrate better on smiting their neighbors since they were no longer looking nervously over their shoulders for Turks in their rear. There had come a change of regime in Constantinople that brought Christendom a few decades of respite from invasion.

The Post-Mehemmed II Ottoman Empire

Following Mehemmed's death in 1481, there occurred another one of the frequent Ottoman succession disputes. The great conqueror's personality had loomed so large during his lengthy (vast numbers would say much too lengthy) reign that he left a gap in the political atmosphere when he departed. Of his two sons, Bayazid was peacefully governing a province in Asia Minor, and seems to have been a mild and fairly pacific man. The younger son, Djem (or Jem, or even Dschem), a bright young man with a gift for poetry, was governor of Karamania. Neither of these two sounds like the sort of replacement their father would have preferred. When he heard the news, Bayazid, the heir, went directly to Constantinople and found a scene of nightmarish horror in progress. It seems that the grand vizier had tried to conceal the sultan's death — a common tactic in Ottoman politics — because he favored Djem over Bayazid and needed time to arrange things. The Janissaries, who favored Bayazid, got wind of this, ran amok, slew the vizier, and started attacking the homes of Jews and Christians. Bayazid managed to placate the rampagers by pardoning them and raising their salaries, but now he had to deal with Djem. The younger son by twelve years, and possibly the favorite of his father, now openly claimed the throne. He offered his brother a compromise plan of dividing the empire between them; this, however, violated Muslim tradition and Ottoman practice, so Bayazid refused and the brothers fought a series of battles in which the elder was victorious.

The Saga of Djem

Djem thereupon became a sort of human ping-pong ball for the rest of his short life. After fleeing to Cairo and mounting a failed attempt to seize Karamania, he bounced over to Rhodes and asked asylum of the Knights. Grand Master d'Aubusson agreed, seeing Djem's possibilities as a bargaining chip in the Knights' delicate relations with the Turks. Bayazid was only too happy to have his brother in residence with the Knights, permanently if possible, and made an agreement with the brethren under which Djem was called a guest of the Knights, and the sultan furnished a sizeable sum of money yearly for his upkeep. Bayazid promised peaceful relations with Rhodes and even sent the Knights of St. John a precious relic: the hand of St. John the Baptist.

Djem was soon sent (ping) to live opulently on an estate owned by the Knights in France, where he was known as the

Grand Turk. Most of the European powers, including the papacy, saw the benefits that possession of this valuable prisoner could bring in their relations with the Ottomans. The popes had never given up the idea of another crusade, and a vague plan developed for the crusaders to take Djem with them and somehow plunk him on the Ottoman throne. The prince himself seems to have promised to liberate much of the territory conquered by his father, and according to one account this even included Constantinople. At length Djem was transferred (pong) to the custody of Pope Innocent VIII, and was received in Rome with great honor and lavish gifts, while the populace turned out in droves to get a glimpse of the famous Grand Turk. He was lodged luxuriously in a Vatican residence and large sums were spent on his comfort.

Meanwhile, the pope was pursuing his plan for the crusade, negotiating both with Djem's former protector, the sultan of Egypt, and with the European powers on the details of the expedition. Bayazid, well informed by the Venetians and his own spies, was sufficiently alarmed to arrange for the Belvedere fountain that supplied Djem's water (as well as the pope's) to be poisoned. Fortunately the would-be poisoner somehow gave himself away while passing through Venice and was caught and sent to Rome for execution in May of 1490. The planning for the crusade continued, until it received a major setback later in the year with the death of the most prominent crusader, the great Hungarian King Matyas Corvinus. This ushered in yet another dispute for the Hungarian throne and the country was temporarily out of the picture as far as the crusade went. The pope himself was ill and embroiled in difficulties with King Ferrante of Naples, rival of the papacy for territorial hegemony in central Italy. (It must always be kept in mind when dealing with this period that the security of the Papal States, then a large area of central Italy, was a major preoccupation of the popes. This was true not only for material and political reasons but because the States were seen as a rampart against the sort of aggression against papal sovereignty and independence that had occurred in the past.)

Sultan Bayazid thought the moment propitious to send ambassadors to the pope with instructions to negotiate Djem's continuing residence in papal custody, and ostensibly to assure themselves that he was in good health (actually the last thing his brother wanted to hear). The Turkish envoy promised that as long as Djem was in papal custody the Turks would not attack any Christian targets; he later qualified this — ominously — to exclude Hungary. The pope, who has been criticized for treating with the Turks at all, sent back word that he would have to consult the other Christian powers before giving a definitive reply. He had already, however, accepted a large installment of the pension that Bayazid promised him for taking care of Djem.

Two years later, shortly before Innocent's own death in 1492, he warned the Turkish emissaries that if the Sultan attacked any Christian country, he would retaliate by unleashing Djem — a prospect Bayazid had been dreading for years. By 1494, Naples and the Papal States, now under the rule of Pope Alexander VI, had patched things up and were preparing to face an invasion by King Charles VIII of France, who was coming to claim the throne of Naples by force. Once in Rome, Charles demanded that the Pope turn Djem over to him, which the pontiff refused to do until a crusade got going. Under threat of invasion by the French army, however, Alexander finally agreed to turn the Grand Turk over to the king's custody. Charles carted the hostage down to Naples with him, evidently seriously — though briefly — considering the launching of a campaign against the Turks. He was soon distracted by the charms of life in Naples, however, and once again the great crusade, so recently and solemnly proclaimed, did not take place. As for Djem, he fell ill on the journey and died quietly on February 25, 1495, after several days of high fever; he was thirty-five years old.

It was immediately whispered about that he had been poisoned, possibly by the pope (who was a Borgia, after all.) The rumor may have been partially based on a supposed letter from the sultan to the pope the previous year in which Bayazid proposed that doing away with Djem would serve both their purposes nicely, and if Alexander would kindly see to it he would receive a large payment for the corpse from the corpse's brother. This document is generally thought to be a forgery, and in any case it seems clear that Djem's death was due to natural causes. It was rumored to have been hastened by his "disorderly life," whatever that may mean, though Italian opinion had never been favorable to the young man. We have many descriptions of his appearance and character, one by the painter Mantegna, which all describe him as cruel and vicious, in part, it seems, because of his facial expressions. Mantegna says he was reputed to have killed four men, and the painter himself apparently witnessed him severely abusing an interpreter. He remains an enigmatic figure, and might even be a tragic one if only we knew more about his true character and personality.

New Ottoman Campaigns

Bayazid, relieved of the threat that had hung over his reign for nearly fourteen years, was now free to proceed against the West once again, if he chose to do so. Although he was not particularly warlike, as sultans go, the habit of gobbling up other people's countries almost absentmindedly was an inveterate Ottoman trait. Bayazid accordingly ordered raids on Hungary, Croatia, the Dalmatian coast, Moldavia, and even Poland, but none of these was a full-scale invasion. His one serious confrontation with a Western power occurred when Venice took over the island of Cyprus in 1489. Even as he prepared for war, with a major shipbuilding operation aimed at bringing him mastery of the seas, he sought to allay suspicion by sending a message of peace to Venice. The Venetian ambassador in Constantinople seems to have forwarded it without comment, although a fellow Venetian had explained to him how ominous it was that the message was not in Turkish but in Latin — meaning, he said, that the sultan would not consider it binding on the Turks.

Somehow the ambassador did not pass this information on to headquarters, and he soon found himself thrown in prison along with the other Venetians in the Ottoman capital as a fleet of nearly three hundred Turkish ships set sail for the Greek port of Lepanto. It was intercepted by a much smaller and disorganized Venetian fleet, which was easily defeated and its brave admiral killed. Lepanto became Turkish, and would become one of the main centers for the Ottoman slave trade. The Turks then went on to wreak havoc on the Venetian territories of the Dalmatian coast, even penetrating into northern Italy not far from the Republic itself.

The sultan then seized nearly all of the smaller holdings that remained to Venice in southern Greece. These changed hands a few times as the Venetian-Turkish conflict went on, until in 1503 a peace treaty was signed that restored some of the captured territory (though not Lepanto) to Venice. Another treaty with Hungary that same year brought peace between the Ottomans and Europe. This respite would last for another seventeen years, while Bayazid turned his attention to Persia. Then an earthquake flattened his capital in 1509 and he had to spend time rebuilding that; in the end, he never again got around to attacking in the west.

Selim the Grim: Really Bad News

Even before the elderly sultan died, his three sons were quarreling over the succession. Toying with the idea of abdicating, Bayazid had designated his eldest son, Ahmad, as his successor. Another son, Selim, opposed his father's plans to such a point that the Sultan unwillingly went to war with him and defeated him. By 1512, all three of his sons were either intriguing for power or in active revolt, but it was Selim who first got to him with his Janissary supporters and forced him to abdicate in his favor. A month later the father, who had asked only to be allowed to retire to his native city, died on the way, universally thought to have been poisoned by Selim.

This next Ottoman ruler would be called "the Grim," and certainly his first moves to solidify his power were grim ones. According to Ottoman custom, both his brothers were executed, as were his five surviving nephews. The story is that as they were being strangled (strangulation was the method generally used to eliminate royal rivals because their blood was not supposed to be shed) Selim complacently listened to their screams from an adjoining room. He was impatient with his staff when they failed to perform according to his expectations, and he expressed this irritation by ordering the execution of anyone who disagreed with him, sometimes doing the job himself.

His grand viziers each lasted such a short time before being executed that they took to carrying their last wills and testaments around with them so as to be ready when they went into the royal presence. One of them once dared to ask the Sultan to give him a little notice if he were to be beheaded, so that he could arrange his affairs. Selim laughed heartily and declared jovially that he had been thinking of killing him for some time but had not found a replacement yet. Oddly enough, there was no shortage of candidates for positions, no matter how brief and precarious they tended to be, in Selim's government. The perks were very considerable, and life at court was anything but boring.

Jihad was high on Selim's agenda, but fortunately for the West he first unleashed it on Shi'ite Muslim heretics, fanatically massacring tens of thousands in Anatolia before marching eastward against Shi'ite Persia. The campaign was a brutal foretaste of what his Western enemies could expect if he began to look in their direction. One historian has written, "beside him, even Mehemmed seems almost genial." On he went, east and south, until he had doubled the size of the already very large Ottoman Empire. Now it included Arabia, with the Muslim holy cities of Mecca and Medina, the caliphate of Cairo, and everything in between Anatolia and Egypt — including the Holy Land. Eastward, the empire stretched to the Indian Ocean. The caliphate of Cairo was particularly important, since that Caliph was also considered the supreme *imam*, the religious head of Islam. Technically the holder of this position was supposed to be a member of the Arab tribe to which Muhammad the Prophet had belonged, a qualification the Ottomans certainly failed to meet. Nobody was about to pick an argument over it with the Grim One, however, so the sultan received the keys to the holy site, the *Kaaba*, in Mecca, and the universal caliphate of the early Islamic period was considered restored in his person.

The Year 1517

Europe watched Selim's progress with growing apprehension, and once again the desperate need for a crusade to meet the inevitable threat from the east became the focus of papal attention. Pope Leo X had made restoring peace among the European powers and launching a crusade the main goals of his pontificate. Soon after his accession in 1512, he was sending money to Rhodes and Hungary, and letters to the rulers of Christendom urging them to make peace and prepare for the crusade. Embroiled in Italian politics and the interests of his family, however, the pope (like the other major rulers) was too distracted when Selim left Constantinople on his eastern campaigns, in the summer of 1516, to take advantage of his absence by attacking his capital. News of the fall of Egypt, though, managed to get Europe's attention.

"If it be true that the Sultan has overcome his ancient foes the Egyptians, it is time that we woke from sleep," wrote the pope, "lest we be put to the sword unawares. If it be not true, why should we not make use of this opportunity?" King Francis I of France went so far as to imagine how the conquered Ottoman Empire would be divided among France, Spain, and the Holy Roman Empire — an early example of the political rather than religious ambitions that would increasingly characterize modern conflicts between Europe and the Ottoman Empire.

The financing of the crusade was the subject of one of the last decrees of the Fifth Lateran Council in 1517, and it almost seemed that the project would actually get off the ground. Of course that never happened. Despite popular enthusiasm in parts of Europe, Henry VIII and Cardinal Wolsey raised objections to papal plans, Emperor Maximilian was willing but the Spanish opposed the crusade taxes, and in Germany, a monk named Martin Luther was lighting the bonfire of the Protestant revolt that would soon engulf most of Europe. Selim died three years later anyway, either of a painful cancer or from the plague, just before his planned revenge on Rhodes, that inconvenient obstacle on the sea route from Cairo to Constantinople. Christendom breathed easier; it was rumored that Selim's son and successor, Suleiman, very unlike his father, was a peaceful and non-threatening sort of Turk, the kind who would leave Europe free to pursue its own wars and conquests.

A Worthy Successor to Mehemmed and Selim

The rumors could not have been more wrong. When Suleiman stepped onto the sixteenth-century stage, he began a spectacular career that represents the high point of Ottoman power, and was anything but peaceful. He was twenty-six years old at his accession in 1520, and during his nearly forty-six year reign he succeeded where even his great-grandfather Mehemmed had failed; Belgrade would fall to him, and Rhodes, Hungary and much more; the Mediterranean would become a Turkish lake. His character differed from that of his father in that he was not excessively cruel, for a sultan, and seemed to have had a genuine concern for justice, for which he became known as the Lawgiver. He was well educated, cultured, patronized the arts, and so impressed Europeans that they called him "the Magnificent" and greatly admired the wonderful realm he ruled. In 1525 the Venetian ambassador gushed, "I know of no state which is happier than this one; it is furnished with all God's gifts . . . no state can be compared with it. May God long preserve the most just of all emperors." Venice was clearly a loyal, even slavish, ally of the Ottomans. Excuses were readily made for Suleiman when he behaved like a Turkish sultan. Yes, people said, he had one of his sons strangled, but that was because of his infatuation with a slave woman who pushed him into it (her fault, no doubt). Yes, he could repress revolt as ruthlessly as his predecessors, but that was mere necessity.

Certainly he took his religious responsibility to wage jihad seriously: as imam and universal caliph it was imperative that he conquer the infidel and spread Islam even into the heart of Europe. He was said to have drawn inspiration from the spectacular career of Alexander the Great, who also sought to unite East and West in a common imperium. Suleiman lost no time getting started, and it was soon clear to observers what his goals were. Yet once again Christendom was paralyzed. The sultan's Western counterpart, Charles V, reigned over the vast Holy Roman Empire, Spain, and the Spanish colonies in the New World. As next-door neighbor to Hungary, he was the ruler most immediately concerned with the Ottomans' next move, but his powerful neighbor on the western side, Francis I, King of France, posed a more immediate threat to Charles' political power and the Italian territories he claimed. Francis would soon make an alliance with the Turks against the Habsburgs, increasing the threat from both directions.

Meanwhile, the Lutheran movement in the German states of Charles' empire had become both a political and a religious revolt, like the related Peasants' War of the early fifteen twenties; both urgently demanded Charles' full attention. In short, with hostilities between the two main political powers on the continent, with Henry VIII of England about to fall for Anne Boleyn, with the Italian states waging mutual war as usual and Venice friendly with the Turks, and with Martin Luther initially urging non-resistance to Turkish attacks on the Catholic emperor, there seemed no possibility of a united response to Turkish aggression. Suleiman would have it all his own way. And he did — for a while.

Main Works Consulted

The Cambridge Modern History. Chapter III, "The Ottoman Empire," by J. B. Bury in vol. I, *The Renaissance.*

Hughes, Philip, Msgr. *The Church in Crisis — the Twenty Great Councils.*

Kinross, Lord. *The Ottoman Empire.*

Pastor, Ludwig von. *History of the Popes*, vols. VII and VIII.

Seven

Jihad at Sea

This next scene might be titled, "Let Many Islands Be Sad," for terror, ruin, and slavery were about to fall upon the isles, large and small, of the Mediterranean Sea. Suleiman's first major maritime target was Rhodes. He had already captured the Hungarian fortress-city of Belgrade, as we will see in the following chapter, and began his siege of Rhodes on June 15, 1522.

Sixteenth-Century Rhodes

By the late 1400s the island had fully recovered from the first Turkish siege, and had become a cosmopolitan haven of prosperity, security, and peace for its inhabitants. The Knights governed justly, used their subjects' Greek language, and did not interfere with their religious practices except to enforce the terms of the Union of Florence. In the countryside, however, it seems that the locals refused to conform in matters such as praying for the pope in their Masses, and wandering Greek monks could be found preaching against the Catholic Church. It is indicative of the harmony between the Knights and the inhabitants that it was the Greek metropolitan and other officials who called the Knights' attention to these rabble-rousing Greek monks, and asked that action be taken against them so that tranquility might be restored. The Knights also provided medical care and food for the poor in times of scarcity, so that materially as well as spiritually this jewel of the Mediterranean was the envy of many — including, of course, the Turks.

During the reign of Selim the Grim, Rhodes too had braced itself for an attack that did not materialize. But there does seem to have been at this time at least one well-organized conspiracy, uncovered through the questioning of a Turkish slave woman, that involved Muslim slaves, foreign merchants, and the Turkish navy. The idea was for the slaves and foreign agents to open the gates when the Turks arrived. The leaders were never discovered, but measures were taken to restrict the movement of slaves (literally, by making them clank about in a ball and chain), make alterations in the security systems, and fortify the defenses once again.

In 1515, delegates from Persia and Egypt arrived, offering to make common cause with the Knights against attack by Selim. The Knights and the Persian and Egyptian representatives signed a treaty, but the arrangement was made null and void the following year when 150 Ottoman ships called at Rhodes. The island prepared for battle, but the great fleet had only come to decant a representative of the sultan with a message for the Grand Master: it informed him of the good news that Selim had just defeated the Egyptians and taken over Syria. Whoever had ears, it continued, had better get the message. Rhodes got it.

The Legendary Siege

In 1521, the new grand master was Philippe Villiers de l'Isle-Adam, who had previously, as grand prior, been sent more than once to Europe to try to collect funds and pledges of material support for Rhodes. He was also a very competent military leader. On October 28, the newly acceded Suleiman sent him a letter congratulating him on his election and pointing out that good relations between them depended on the grand master's attitude. He was therefore cordially invited to congratulate the sultan for his victory at Belgrade where, Suleiman added, "the edge of Our terrible sword" had fallen on "all who dared to resist us." Brother Philippe fired back a letter saying he had understood his majesty's meaning and that his peace proposals were "as agreeable to me as they are unpleasant to Kurtoglu." This Kurtoglu was a Turkish admiral — a former pirate — who had recently tried and failed to capture l'Isle-Adam, and had then attempted to plunder two merchant ships. But "this pirate," as the grand master calls him, was forced to flee the scene when the galleys of the Order went after him.

Both leaders knew where they stood, though they continued to exchange courteous letters full of thinly veiled threats. Meanwhile preparations on Rhodes continued; Venice objected when l'Isle-Adam hired mercenaries from Venetian-held Crete, for fear its Turkish allies might be irritated. The grand master did it anyway. Finally, on June 15, 1522, the great Ottoman fleet of two hundred ships, some forty thousand sailors and twenty-five thousand marines sailed into view, commanded by pirate-turned-admiral Kurtoglu; more men and ships were to come later from the Asian coast. The Knights at the Corpus Christi Mass when the news came, and did not leave to take up their posts until the Mass was finished. By the time the full Turkish force had landed and camped around the city, it may have numbered as many as two hundred thousand. In the fortress of Rhodes there were three hundred Knights and the same number of armed servants, also members of the Order. There also were forty-five hundred Rhodian soldiers and the four hundred Cretan mercenaries. It goes without saying that no army arrived from Europe.

The siege lasted into September and the details are often confusing. The sultan, who was present, became increasingly irritated at the delay and ordered an intensification of mining operations under the walls — a major feature of this siege. The Rhodians had an expert who was able to detect many of the underground mines so that countermines could be dug to allow gases to escape and Knights to descend and fight the miners underground. On September 23, Suleiman issued an ultimatum to his troops: they would take Rhodes and have three days of plunder or they would die on the walls and go to Paradise. The following day such a massive assault took place that the Janissaries were able to take one of the towers, and some of the Knights found themselves outside besieging their own captured walls. They were able to use secret passages, however, to get back inside and take the Janissaries by surprise. This little victory seems to have produced a pause in the proceedings by late afternoon. Over fifteen thousand Turks were said to have fallen, some of them dispatched by the women of Rhodes, who alternated between providing bread and wine to the defenders and throwing stones and boiling water at the enemy.

Suleiman, frustrated, ordered the execution of two of his officers but was persuaded to pardon them; instead he took his annoyance out on the bumbling Kurtoglu, who was sentenced to be beaten on the deck of his ship for not taking part in the attack and for allowing Rhodian ships to enter and leave the port. For a few days following September 24 there was a lull in the fighting, and it is possible that the Turks were considering withdrawing. At some point during this period a man named Blas Diez, servant of Grand Chancellor Andrea d'Amaral, was caught sending messages to the enemy describing how bad the situation was inside the walls and urging them to attack in force. Another traitor had earlier been caught doing the same thing, but Diez's master d'Amaral was known for his long-standing antipathy to the Grand Master. Both were condemned to death, though d'Amaral denied his guilt to the end, even under torture. He was stripped of his habit by the general chapter of the Order and given up to the secular authorities to be beheaded.

The Turks, heartened by the information given by the traitors, made a renewed effort to breach the most damaged parts of the fortress. Meanwhile the defenders used rubble to build a new bulwark, even using parts of still-intact buildings for material. A few volunteers continued to trickle in from outlying parts of the island and elsewhere, but not from the only countries that could have helped significantly: the great powers of Europe. Disease spread among the Turks outside the walls as winter approached, and at one point an attack was repulsed, causing three thousand enemy casualties, with the aid of what seemed a miraculous downpour of rain. It was St. Andrew's feast day and the Rhodians attributed it to him.

The sultan's army now tried psychological warfare in the form of messages sent on arrows, and agents who sneaked into the town sapping morale by warning that failure to surrender would mean that no one would be spared when the island was conquered. This caused some of the citizens to mention to the grand master the possibility of surrender. Despite his opposition to any such idea, he promised to consider it. He met with his men to go over the situation. Every soldier still living had been wounded; the food was gone, and ammunition had been used up; the people would perish along with the Knights if they did not give up. Then came a letter from Suleiman formally requesting the surrender of Rhodes. White flags were hoisted on both sides, and discussions with the Turks began. Suleiman's offer was brief: surrender Rhodes and the Knights would be allowed to leave; continue fighting and face the extermination of the whole population and the destruction of the island. But now many of the people, not trusting the Turks, declared that they would rather die fighting than surrender and suffer the fate of Belgrade, where no one had been spared. D'Amaral asked for more time to consult with the citizens, but Suleiman's answer was another attack on the walls. The Order's negotiator again went out to meet the Sultan, this time accompanied by two Rhodian Greeks. Cutting short all attempts at bargaining, Suleiman dictated terms on December 20, 1522: except for a small number of Janissaries, the army would pull back and stay out of the city for twelve days, during which all who wanted to leave could do so unmolested. Those who did not leave within the twelve-day period would have three years after the inevitable conquest in which to change their minds and go. There would be no plundering of homes or churches, and taxes would not be collected for five years, nor would the *devşirme*.

It sounded too good to be true. It was. The unruly Bashi-Bazouks, lusting for plunder, began sneaking towards the city from their camp, and on Christmas Eve, while the people were in church, they broke into the town. Without weapons, the populace was at their mercy: beaten, raped, tortured to reveal supposed hidden treasure, even the hospital patients manhandled. Churches were defiled and relics destroyed, with even the graves of the grand masters desecrated in the hunt for treasure. The call of the *muezzin* sounded from a tower on Christmas Day. The grand master went to meet with the sultan and agreed to the surrender.

Suleiman himself then entered the city, inspecting what was now his palace and praying to Allah in the cathedral, which would then become a mosque, like nearly all the churches of

Rhodes. On New Year's Day, 1523, the flag of the Knights was lowered after two hundred years, never to fly in Rhodes again. In the harbor, fifty ships loaded the Knights and as many Rhodians as wanted to leave and were able to get a place on the vessels. Some five thousand people departed, for an unknown destination. The Knights, along with many of the Rhodians, finally settled in 1530 on Malta, where we will soon meet them again. Though Suleiman did not know it, he had made a colossal blunder in allowing them to go free.

More Really Bad News: Barbarossa

Suleiman always thought big, and in the same decade that saw the fall of Rhodes and the Turkish assault on Hungary, described in the next chapter, his plans came to include mastery of the entire Mediterranean Sea. By creating a navy far superior to that of the Emperor Charles V, he would be in a position to attack the coasts of any European country with impunity. The very man who could make this dream come true was soon to make the great sultan's acquaintance.

Kheir-ed-din Barbarossa (from his red beard) was the son of a Christian apostate and the widow of a Greek priest from the island of Lesbos. A Turkish subject, he became a corsair and merchant operating mainly off the coasts of Muslim North Africa, which had come under nominal Turkish suzerainty following the conquest of Egypt by Selim I. He first strengthened the coastal defenses and established good relations with the Arabs further inland. He then sent a ship carrying valuable gifts to Selim to make his exploits known in Constantinople. Impressed, the sultan made him provincial governor of Africa, and sent him a horse, banner, sword, soldiers and arms to go with the job.

Barbarossa was now an established Ottoman official, but it was not until 1533, after Selim had died and Suleiman had turned his attention to naval affairs, that the pirate admiral received a summons from Constantinople. Suleiman had heard of his battles with the Habsburg navy and was impressed; he also remembered that the great Genoese Admiral Andrea Doria was in charge of the Habsburg fleet that had more than once gotten the better of the Turks. Now he needed an Ottoman Doria.

Barbarossa made a splashy entrance into Constantinople, with forty decorated ships laden with gifts for Suleiman, ranging from gold and jewels to African lions and a large number of Christian girls for his harem. The officers who accompanied the corsair chief were put to work supervising the sultan's shipbuilding project, a job they performed so well that within a few months a world-class fleet was ready to sail against the West with Barbarossa as admiral-in-chief. The new admiral favored an alliance with the French against the Habsburgs in order to counterbalance imperial naval power, and such an agreement was negotiated a few years later. Meanwhile, Barbarossa pursued his project of enforcing Ottoman rule along the whole North African coast, with himself as overlord. He began in 1534 with Tunisia, at that time a largely independent territory embroiled in a war over succession to the throne. The admiral quickly annexed it to the Ottoman Empire, and it now served as a convenient base from which the Turkish fleet could attack Malta, Sicily, and other nearby targets.

The Slaves of the Barbary Coast

We have already seen the extent to which Muslim powers depended on slave labor and routinely captured, bought, and sold hundreds of thousands of slaves throughout their empires.

Due to the extent and longevity of the Ottoman Empire, the total number enslaved is staggering, though it seems that so far we only have figures for certain areas, one of which is the North African coast known as Barbary. This fringe of the Ottoman Empire was a conglomeration of Muslim principalities ruled by either Arabs left over from the original Islamic conquest of Christian Africa, or Muslim converts like the Berbers. The Moors expelled from Spain in 1492 by Ferdinand and Isabella were scattered along the coast opposite Spain, burning for revenge, and the Ottoman presence increased in the sixteenth century thanks to Barbarossa.

For Christian Europe, Barbary was synonymous with slavery: from the numerous ports, Muslim pirates and corsairs cruised the coasts of Europe and its islands, often penetrating far inland in their search for plunder and slaves. Men, women, and children were taken back to Barbary where they were used for slave labor, as rowers of galleys, or — in the case of younger women and many children and young men — to serve the depraved appetites of Muslim men able to afford them. A recent historian of the subject has calculated that between 1530 — about when Barbarossa hit his stride — and 1780, the Barbary Muslims enslaved at least a million, possibly as many as a million and a quarter, European Christians.[4] The total equals or exceeds the number of black Africans shipped as slaves to the Americas, and that is leaving out the vast numbers of Christians enslaved throughout the former Byzantine Empire as well as the Asian territories taken over by the Ottomans. A single raid could often collect as many slaves from Europe as would be shipped from Africa to America during an entire year. From

[4] It should be noted that North African slave-taking on a large scale went back to the original Muslim conquest; it was the stimulus for the growth of religious orders devoted to the ransom of captives during the Middle Ages. Detailed statistics, however, exist only for the more modern period.

Barbary, the slaves not needed by the locals could be sold or transported to the east, with many thousands needed to man the Ottoman fleet, as well as the corsair vessels. The plight of the galley slaves was the most inhumane of all — made worse because they were forced to row their ships in campaigns to kill or enslave other Christians.

A Saint in Chains

St. Vincent de Paul knew firsthand what slaves in Barbary endured, and the story of his own experiences provides a glimpse of their plight. In 1607, as a young man on a routine voyage between two French cities, he was wounded by an arrow when his French ship came under corsair attack and was captured. Even though their French vessel had to surrender, he wrote, "these criminals, who are worse than tigers" were not satisfied. "In the first outburst of their rage they cut our captain into a hundred thousand bits because they had lost one of their best men, besides four or five convicts whom our men had killed." On the rest of the journey to North Africa he observed the activities of the corsairs as they looted their way back to port at Tunis, where there were already seven thousand or more Christian slaves. There he and his fellow passengers were advertised to have come from a Spanish ship, not French (the French were on good trading terms with the pirates even though their own ships were being seized). St. Vincent was then put up for sale, in chains:

> The merchants came to see us, for all the world just like people come to the sale of a horse or an ox, making us open our mouths to see our teeth, feeling our sides, examining our wounds, making

us walk, trot and run, making us carry weights and fight so as to gauge the strength of each, as well as a thousand other forms of brutality.

The young captive was first bought by a fisherman but did not do well at sea and soon was resold to an alchemist — an old Muslim engaged both in trying to transmute metals and in the more practical science of pharmacy. St. Vincent learned much from assisting this old man, though he disapproved of the tricks the clever mountebank also developed to fool the gullible. In 1604, a new treaty between King Henry IV and the sultan was supposed to bring the release of all Christian slaves and Christian goods, but by 1606 only a few dozen had been freed and Vincent was not among them.

When his old master died, St. Vincent was resold to a French Catholic priest who had first been captured and then had apostatized in order to gain his freedom. He lived in the country with three wives — of whom only one seems to have been Muslim — and used St. Vincent, now twenty-six, as a field laborer. The work was as hard as the heat was extreme, but he never ceased to have confidence in the Blessed Virgin, to whom he had always been devoted. Two of the wives were attracted by Vincent's conversation and hymn-singing, and soon the Muslim wife was telling her husband that she no longer believed in her religion and that he had been wrong to abandon his. Smitten by his conscience, the apostate determined to escape, together with Vincent. After ten months of preparation, the two managed to cross the sea to France in June 1607. The apostate was reconciled with the Church and entered a strict monastery. (We are not told what became of the wives.) As for St. Vincent, he would later make missionary work to the slaves one of the aspects of his multi-form apostolate of charity.

Muslim Slave-Trading Raids

For the people of the European coasts and island, the material damage done by the pirates was grim enough. Coastal merchants were ruined, shipping stagnated, settlements were depopulated and everything in them hopelessly damaged. As for the plight of the captives in Barbary, numerous accounts have survived, along with pathetic letters that many of the slaves were able to write home. The Trinitarians and other religious dedicated to ransoming slaves were overwhelmed with the magnitude of their task, and many priests voluntarily went to North Africa in order to minister to the despairing Christians who might otherwise have lost their Faith. Under Barbarossa, the shipbuilding whiz, corsair fleets grew tremendously and the damage they were able to inflict, as well as the number of slaves they collected, greatly increased. Suleiman was rapidly achieving his goal of supremacy in the entire Mediterranean and its coastal regions.

A harrowing account of a raid on a Sicilian village describes the lightning attacks of the pirates, the pillaging, the seizing of women and children, and the rapid departure of the ships. One or two days later the corsairs would often return flying white flags, which signaled a willingness to bargain for the release of the captives. Relatives would be allowed aboard — partly in order to frighten them with a preview of what was in store for their loved ones if their ransom was not paid, as brutal Moors dragged terrified wives and children before their spouses and parents. For Christians, the possibility of forcible conversion to Islam, or simply the loss of the Faith, was the worst prospect of all. Needless to say, even impoverished fishermen would try everything to scrape together the ransom money, often resorting to the loan sharks — with us then as now — swarming about such scenes. The ransomed captives were the lucky ones; sometimes the entire population of a village was captured, with little hope of ransom.

Under Barbarossa, the destruction that always accompanied corsair raids became more systematic: fortresses, houses, crops, and anything else of use to the Christian enemy were tactically destroyed. Other systematic damage, of a kind which could have had no tactical purpose, included the desecration of churches and shrines. The Muslims stabbed holy pictures, spit on images, and otherwise defiled sacred things. A contemporary Italian poet wrote of "the outrage done to God . . . the crucifixes and the images of the saints, of God, of the Madonna and the Holy Sacrament," describing how the holy things were mocked, pierced with arrows, thrown to the ground, and stabbed with daggers, before being burned. Ordinary pirates would not have wasted time defacing sacred objects when there were more profitable things to do. Only a festering hatred of Christianity can account for this wanton desecration.

Modern historians have portrayed the massive slave-trading operations, as well as unprovoked Turkish aggression everywhere, as simply the same sort of thing Westerners had themselves always done to their enemies.[5] It is true that slavery survived longer in Europe than is often realized, though it lacked both the character and scale of the Turkish system. There were also examples of retaliatory raids by Western corsairs taking Muslim (and often fellow Christian) captives into slavery, but

[5] The modern historian loathes moral judgments, and even one of the most recent historians of slavery in Barbary almost apologizes for using the term "barbarian," explaining that it is an adjective applied to the Turks by their contemporaries.

both the slavery and the slave trading were on a much smaller scale than the Turkish, and both had largely died out by the early modern period.

There is another important distinction to keep in mind here. Westerners certainly enslaved large numbers of Africans in often-cruel conditions, and Western soldiers could be as brutal and sadistic as Turkish soldiers. However, the Church strived to undo or temper the injustice wherever possible. In the South American slave port of Cartagena, for example, as soon as the slaves began to arrive they were met by Jesuit missionaries like St. Peter Claver and Fr. Sandoval, and treated as human beings — often for the first time in their lives, including their early lives in Africa. Sandoval was the author of the first treatise calling for the abolition of slavery, and the popes regularly condemned it. When the Spanish created an empire in the Americas, one of the first concerns of the government and the Church was to explore the question of the human rights of the indigenous population and spell them out in documents. That rights were often violated cannot be denied, but the Church and the Spanish monarchs continued to insist on their recognition.

In contrast, unless some new information is unearthed to contradict everything we know of the Ottoman Empire, there never was an antislavery movement throughout its history. The very idea of some Western pirate presenting, say, Charles V with a thousand Muslim girls for his enjoyment, as Barbarossa presented Christian girls to Suleiman, is ludicrous because of Catholic moral teaching on both sex and the rights of women. It is also curious how silent historians are on the lot of Christian women slaves. The indignation freely expressed by historians of the African slave trade does not seem to extend to the millions of Christian women enslaved by the Muslims. Only a few of these women — those hardy souls who somehow came to positions of power within the harem — ever seem to attract attention. This curious double standard applied to Christian and Muslim behavior deserves scholarly exploration.

Meanwhile, that same Charles V who did not have a harem was preparing for war.

The West Fights Back

Emperor Charles V determined to attack the haunts of the corsairs in North Africa as part of his commitment to the struggle against the Turks. He made of this expedition a crusade, with the blessing and assistance of Pope Paul III, who sent ships of the papal fleet to join the imperial force. Charles himself made a pilgrimage to Our Lady of Montserrat before leaving Spain, and had an image of a crucifix hung on the flagship of the fleet. "The Crucified Savior," he told his men, "shall be our captain."

The fleet that sailed on June 13, 1535 included over four hundred ships under the command of Andrea Doria, as well as many imperial troops; its goal was to capture Tunis. The siege of the major fortress would be a long one. At one point Charles promised pardon to all apostate Christians serving in the enemy army who deserted to the Christian side; many did. After a hard and costly fight, a huge ship of the Knights of St. John was able to fire the decisive blow against the walls. Most of Barbarossa's ships were captured, and he himself was preparing for a land battle against the imperial forces at Tunis when twenty thousand Christian captives within the city (led by a Knight of St. John) revolted and turned the tide in favor of the Christian army. Unfortunately, Charles had promised his men they would be allowed to sack the city; the grim acts they carried out on its defenseless population were unworthy of followers of the Crucified.

The emperor and his victory were cheered all over Europe (except, probably, in the palace of Francis I), and Charles began to dream of proceeding to Constantinople. Barbarossa had survived, however, and was by no means finished. He fled to a port where he had more ships waiting and quickly made an attack on the Balearic Islands off the Spanish coast before anyone could stop him. He cleverly flew Spanish and Italian flags so his ships would receive a welcome when they landed. Too late, the hapless residents of the town of Mahón on Minorca saw their town sacked and thousands of Christians taken into slavery.

In 1536, when Barbarossa again visited the sultan, he was asked to build another two hundred ships for an assault on Italy, and the following year the admiral was heading west again with his new fleet. He first landed at Otranto (poor city, twice victim of the Turks) and wreaked havoc on the whole coast. Fortunately for Italy, further Turkish operations there had been predicated on the cooperation of Francis I. Fickle Francis, however, changed his mind and made a truce with Emperor Charles; he was thus unavailable to help the Turks despoil Italy. So that the expedition would not be profitless, the sultan ordered operations against Venice, which had been attacking Turkish ships in retaliation for the new favor now being shown by the Turks to French merchants. Venice got the better of the first couple of engagements, so Barbarossa took revenge on the Venetian islands in the Aegean Sea: sacking them, taking their ships, and capturing thousands more slaves. These he dressed up in fancy clothes to meet the sultan, and made them march in procession, carrying the stolen loot, into the royal presence. He knew how to make an impression.

The Many Islands

There are more islands than one can count in the Mediterranean, some of them, in the eastern half of the sea, only large rocks with no inhabitants, some insular paradises like Rhodes and Crete, supporting sizeable populations. All of them were at the mercy of Muslim naval terrorists, and even after the Ottoman fleet suffered major defeats in the sixteenth century and later, their hold on many of the islands continued well into the nineteenth century. Patmos got off easy. This "holy island" in the Aegean is the place to which St. John the Evangelist was banished by the Roman Emperor Domitian, and where he had the revelations he recorded in the Book of Revelation. The cavern in which the revelations occurred can still be visited, and still breathes forth a sacred atmosphere that is unforgettable.

The island had first endured Muslim raids from the Arabs in the seventh century. In the early sixteenth century it was part of the dominion of the Knights of St. John, but after the fall of Rhodes it was occupied by the Ottoman Turks. It seems the main hardship inflicted on its people was taxation, though a document in the monastery library records that "some sixty Turkish galliots [ships] came and enslaved all our people two, three, and four times, and deprived them of their goods." Perhaps because of its small size (or due to the protection of St. John) it seems to have escaped the attention of the great powers for long periods, during which it went its own way, though it was actually ceded to the Turks in 1830 in return for their evacuation of a larger Greek island. Through it all, the great monastery protecting the holy cave survived, and the island is now Greek.

The capital of Crete, Chania, which had been taken over by Venice, suffered corsair raids in 1537 and 1538, and fell to the

Turks after a long siege in the following century. Heraklion, the modern capital of the island, suffered many Turkish attacks, though its Venetian-built defenses held out until 1669. The island of Santorini fell to the Turks in 1537, but the people and monks were determined to preserve their Christianity and pass it on to their children. The monks of the Monastery of Elias set up a secret schoolroom in which they taught the Greek language and Christian doctrine to children and kept the morale of the people alive. The island of Delos was largely uninhabited but contained an archaeological treasure trove: large-scale ruins of a great sanctuary to which the ancient Greeks had made pilgrimages. Ironically, following the Greek defeat of another great assault from the east, that of the ancient Persians, Delos had become the repository for funds contributed by the various city-states for defense against another attack. The Persians never tried again; when the Turks came instead, there was no treasury of Delos left to finance Greek resistance. The Turks occupied even empty Delos, using it as a pirate base and looting the marble and any other useful material from the irreplaceable ruins for their own purposes.

One by one fell the islands, whether independent Greek communities or Venetian holdings. Meanwhile, the Turks had not forgotten Malta.

Suleiman's Blunder at Malta

The year was 1564, and the Knights of St. John were settled in their new home on the island of Malta. They had been far from idle since Suleiman allowed them to leave Rhodes. We have already seen the Knights of St. John playing a major role in the capture of Tunis. Another Knight once successfully defended the fortress of Nice, even though the city itself had fallen, and other members of the Order were to be found in the thick of whatever action was going on between the Western powers and the Ottomans. Suleiman was fed up. The successes of the Knights constantly reminded him that he himself had allowed them to get where they were, and the very existence of their new island fortress, between Sicily and the African coast, was an obstacle to his full control of the Mediterranean. Furthermore, one of his daughters by a favorite wife had been nagging him to move against the Knights. It is said that she received very vocal support from the women of the harem when the Knights intercepted a large merchant vessel full of luxury goods in which the women had invested. Other advisors reminded Suleiman of the many Muslim slaves in Malta, whom it was his duty to liberate. At seventy, the sultan thought he was too old to lead the campaign in person, (though the grand master who was to foil his plan was the same age) but he had a first-class military and naval staff — or so he thought.

Barbarossa had died in 1546, not cut down by a Christian sword or strangled in a palace intrigue, as one might have expected, but of natural causes in his palace in Constantinople, and at a ripe old age at that. He was succeeded by Dragut, his protégé, now eighty years old but still going strong as a chief advisor to Suleiman. Dragut had enjoyed an extremely successful career raiding coastal Europe and capturing North African and Aegean strongholds from the Christians, so taking a small island was nothing to him. Still, with the Knights of St. John it was always better to be on the safe side, and Suleiman was taking no chances this time. The expedition was therefore put under the command of two men, one for the navy and one for the land forces, but both were to consult Dragut and another experienced corsair and do nothing against their advice. It sounded like a foolproof scheme.

In March of 1565, an armada of some 150 warships, plus supply ships and other vessels, sailed out of Constantinople, carrying about 40,000 men. On Malta, Grand Master Jean Parisot de la Valette made his preparations. He had been a Knight for fifty years, had fought the Turks at Rhodes, and had later survived a year of Turkish captivity as a galley slave. A degree of laxity had crept into Malta, as it had periodically done in Rhodes, and after his election in 1557 de la Valette had made it a priority to restore strict discipline. There were fewer than 600 Knights and servants-at-arms on Malta, and they had to man three fortified sites. The Order had suffered from the Reformation; it was suppressed in Protestant states, and in England the brethren refused to follow the example of many other orders in capitulating to Henry VIII, and so had to flee the country, five dying martyrs. The number of new recruits was thus reduced. Besides Brethren, however, there were on Malta 1,200 mercenaries from Italy and Spain, and 3,000 Maltese militiamen. Still, even counting other residents, galley slaves, and 600 soldiers who would later be sent by Pope Pius IV, the total was only about 6,000 men — outnumbered six or seven to one by the Turks.

Charles V was dead and his son, Philip II, King of Spain, had promised both ships and men. He had already lost many ships to the Turks, however, and the sailors of his newly equipped fleet needed more training and experience before he could risk a difficult campaign outside home waters. As at Rhodes, the Knights were on their own. As the enemy fleet approached, the grand master addressed his men in the famous words, "Today our faith is at stake — whether the Gospel must yield to the

Koran. God is asking for the lives which we pledged to Him at our profession. Happy are those who may sacrifice their lives." The Turks first assaulted the new and small fort of St. Elmo, at the end of a narrow strip of land projecting into the sea. There was some disagreement among the Turks as to whether they should tackle such an exposed position, but in the end they did it. From mid-May to mid-June they hurled waves of men against the fort. They had captured a Knight whom they tortured in order to extract information about the best place to attack; only later did they realize that the Knight had deceived them and it was the wrong place. Besides the usual Janissaries and the frontline riff-raff, sources give prominence in this battle to the role of the dervishes. These religious enthusiasts were once again used to fire up the troops with frenzied preaching, fanatical cries, and martial music. (It was said that if the music stopped, the Janissaries did too, fearing something amiss.) The three hundred men inside St. Elmo were periodically reinforced during the night, to replace those who died during the day. One brave brother who fell, mortally wounded in the chest, urged a comrade to leave him and help others because he was dead anyway. Then he dragged himself to the chapel to expire at the foot of the altar.

On June 21 the Knights held their Corpus Christi procession, which must have recalled to the grand master the beginning of the siege of Rhodes on that very date. The following day the Turks sent in most of their army, and the fort fell. The Turks lost 8,000 men to gain the ruins of that small fort; the defenders lost 1,500, including 120 Knights. A few Maltese escaped by swimming, and nine Knights were said to have been taken alive. After the battle the Turks decapitated each corpse and nailed it to a wooden cross before pushing it into the water. These arrived on the shore where the main Christian force was, and ignited a fury among them. The grand master ordered the Turkish prisoners beheaded and had the heads fired from cannon into the Turkish camp. It was June 23, the Feast of St. John, patron of the Order. Dragut had been mortally wounded, and was quickly removed from the scene so as not to shake the soldiers' morale. He lived just long enough to hear the news of the fall of St. Elmo, though not long enough to see the end of the Turkish fiasco.

Now the demoralized Turks had the main forts and towns of Malta still to deal with, as the summer heat intensified and they became sick from the well water that the Knights had poisoned. Several hundred Christian reinforcements had arrived, and de la Valette was busy laying iron chains underwater across the inlets. Turkish attempts to cut them were met by expert Maltese swimmers who fought them under the sea. A young Algerian Muslim leader turned up, self-confident and brashly criticizing the Ottoman performance at St. Elmo. He was allowed to attack his way, and ended up losing most of his men. Into August the Turks assaulted the various Maltese bastions. Supplies were short within the walls and everyone was fighting — including, as at Rhodes, the women, who poured boiling water down on the attackers. On and on it went. The grand master was urged to draw back to the great fortress of St. Angelo, but that would mean abandoning the Maltese women and children in the villages and he would not do it. In order to eliminate the temptation, in fact, he blew up the bridge that led to St. Angelo.

The Turks were suffering too, as Christian corsairs intercepted their supply ships and fever and disease still plagued them, with nothing like the expert medical care, in which the Knights specialized, available to them. Soon it was September, and the weather was now threatening. The leaders of the army and the navy began to quarrel, with the army chief willing to spend the winter on Malta and the naval commander anxious to get his fleet away from such a vulnerable site with no maintenance facilities.

At last the Christian reinforcements arrived, ten thousand of them from all over Europe, on Spanish ships that sailed past St. Angelo firing their guns in salute. It was September 8, Feast of the Nativity of Our Lady. The Turkish troops were quickly embarked, then disembarked as their leaders realized the Christians had fooled them and the force was not as large as it had seemed. It was too late, however; the men had become further demoralized, and when the Christian soldiers attacked they broke and ran. Finally the Ottoman fleet departed on a thousand-mile voyage back to Constantinople, with but a quarter of its 40,000 men.

Suleiman was in a towering rage when they arrived, swearing that he would take Malta himself in the spring. Meanwhile, de la Valette had lost 250 brethren, some 2,500 mercenaries, and 7,000 Maltese men, women, and children. The new pontiff, Pope St. Pius V, offered to make the grand master a cardinal, but he refused because it would mean visiting Rome and he needed to stay and rebuild Malta. With contributions from all over the West, he was able to build a monastery, hospital, church, and other buildings that recalled those of his beloved Rhodes; much of the work was well underway or completed before he died in 1568.

Suleiman did not return in the spring. We shall see why presently.

Main Works Consulted

Bradford, Ernle. *The Shield and the Sword.*

Carroll, Warren H. *A History of Christendom*, vol. IV.

Coste, Pierre, C.M. *The Life and Works of St. Vincent de Paul*, vol. I. Quotations taken from pp. 28–29.

Davis, Robert C. *Christian Slaves and Muslim Masters.* Quotation from p. 41.

Kinross, Lord. *The Ottoman Empire.*

Pastor, Ludwig von. *History of the Popes*, vols. IX and XI.

Pavlidis, Vangelis. *Rhodes 1306–1522: A Story.*

Seward, Desmond. *The Monks of War.*

Walsh, William Thomas. *Philip II.*

Eight

Hungary's Passion

All of Europe had been following the progress of the Turks through the Balkans, with those countries closest to the war zone paying closest attention. The papacy and the other states of Italy, the Holy Roman Empire, and the Mediterranean islands were all on edge as the sixteenth century dawned, but most in danger was Hungary. As the geographical gateway to Western Europe for any successful invader, its conquest would pose a deadly peril for the rest of the continent. The country had long suffered from Turkish raids and attacks on its borders, and the occupation of its entire territory was a real possibility. Reports reached the Hungarians of what Turkish rule had meant for their southern neighbors, and that news was not encouraging.

The Balkan Balance Sheet

The physical damage done to the Balkan states by the Ottomans was tremendous. The Turks destroyed towns, fortresses, defensive walls, farmhouses, and crops. They enslaved untold numbers of captives, murdered countless others — both combatants and civilians — and looted everywhere they went. They took livestock for their own use and to prevent its use by the conquered population. The lands of owners who had fled or been killed were turned over either to Turkish colonizers or Christian vassals loyal to their overlords — especially those willing to turn Muslim, which happened more frequently in Bosnia and southern Albania than elsewhere. Once subdued, Christians who refused to apostatize were subject to the usual poll tax and the various means used by the Turks to reinforce the humiliation of the *dhimmi*. This varied according to region and the local ruler's attitude. The dress restrictions, such as wearing yellow, that the Turks imposed in Asia, Bulgaria, and other areas do not seem to have been enforced in most of the Balkans, though other restrictions were. Perhaps most harrowing of all was the inexorable collection of hundreds of thousands of Balkan children for the infamous *devşirme*.

Certainly the overall picture was grim, and Hungary and other near neighbors of the Ottoman Balkans braced themselves to resist their own enslavement. They were to have a respite of several decades, however, due to the internal developments within the Turkish realm that we reviewed in chapter seven. One might think that the blessed respite would have been used to establish impregnable defenses and international alliances everywhere, and that the memory of the near escape of Italy would have moved that country's many republics and monarchies to make common cause (and intensive preparations) for the next wave of invasion. Of course it didn't happen that way, and this next scene will be one of almost unrelieved tragedy.

Hungary in the Sixteenth Century

The state of Hungary at this time is all the more depressing to consider when we recall the kingdom's great Catholic past. The pagan Magyar tribes that had struck terror into Europe in the ninth and tenth centuries had, through the efforts of heroic missionaries and martyrs, been largely converted to Catholicism by the year 1000. In that year, the great King St. Stephen received the apostolic crown from Pope Sylvester, an event from which Hungary's history as a great Catholic country dates. St. Stephen's wife was beatified and their son Imre canonized, as was King Laszlo, who died in 1095 just before he was to lead the First Crusade. Canonized royal daughters included St. Elizabeth of Hungary and St. Margaret; in all, some twenty-six members of the royal house of Arpád were canonized or beatified. If ever there was an exemplary Catholic state with an obviously Catholic political vocation, it was this one.

By the sixteenth century, however, much of that early faith and fervor had waned, and this growing indifference to the precepts of religion was reflected in the increasingly violent state of Hungarian society and the abuse of the most defenseless classes. The three disasters that struck Hungary in the 1500s were the Reformation, which struck at its very soul; the often predatory measures taken by the Austrian Habsburgs to make Hungary part of their empire, which threatened its political independence; and the invasions of the Turks, which largely destroyed its national life.

Historians naturally view these developments from radically different points of view, depending on their own mentality. Protestant and some secular writers see the Reformation as one of those Good Things of history. They applaud the various arrangements made during this period giving full rights to all religions, and condemn the efforts of the Counter-Reformation to restore Hungary to Catholic unity. The idea of national independence is also, to the modern mind, one of those obviously Good Things that in Hungary's case justified revolt against Habsburg rule and collaboration with the Turks against it. Ottoman "tolerance," especially for Protestants, is overstressed, while some undeniable German atrocities associated with the final expulsion of the Turks are too strongly emphasized. Only a few timid Catholic historians venture to point out that since the Faith was the most precious possession of Hungary — its very identity as a nation — as well the bond of unity among its people, that Faith should have informed all of national life as well as resistance to Ottoman Turks.

The problem is that the situation within Hungary was never simple. The Turks were always wrong, since they had no business being there in the first place. The Austrians should have helped much more than they did to drive out the Turks, and respected much more the political traditions of a fellow ancient Catholic country instead of treating it as merely a piece of future Austrian real estate, as they often did. The Hungarians should have put their religion first in everything, cooperating with the sometimes-obnoxious Austrians against their common enemies and making accommodations where necessary to preserve the Catholic Hungarian kingdom. They should also have treated the lower classes with Christian charity and justice, instead of brutalizing them to a degree shocking even by comparison with the worst abuses of peasants at certain periods of Western European history. At the end of the fifteenth century, a famous Franciscan preacher, Pelbárt of Temesvár, had tried in vain to arouse the consciences of the ruling classes: "You are holding orgies in your palaces, while the poor people . . . are dying of hunger." It was said that the horses of gentlemen were better off than their serfs. Then as now, however, fallen human nature got in the way of ideal courses of action.

The Ottomans Strike While the King Plays

It was 1520 and that nice young sultan, Suleiman, was on the Turkish throne. The monarch of Hungary, Lajos II, was sixteen years old and had been king since the age of ten. As the son of the previous king, who was a foreigner and neither competent nor popular, Lajos inherited a country just recovering from a massive rebellion that had, ironically, started as a crusade against the Turks. Cardinal Bakócz, an ambitious man who had failed in his bid to be elected pope and perhaps now yearned for at least military glory, issued a summons to the crusade in 1514 that was answered by masses of the common people, eager to take up arms against the enemy. The nobility was strongly opposed to the whole enterprise, so the cardinal made the mistake of putting a soldier named Dózsa in command of the rag-tag army; having shaped it up, this adventurer disobeyed orders to move south and engage the Turks, and instead turned the expedition into a great peasant rebellion that was eventually put down with extreme brutality, exercised upon the innocent as well as the guilty.

Young King Lajos has been variously described as empty-headed and pleasure-seeking or talented-but-depraved. Either way, he does not sound like a promising antagonist to the undeniably gifted Suleiman. There had been a truce between Hungary and the Ottomans for some years, though Turkish raiders continued to harass the southern borders and besiege the frontier fortresses; particularly irritating to Suleiman was the continued heroic resistance of the fortresses of Szabács and Belgrade. He resolved to take these by force, and perhaps hoping to provoke a reaction from the Hungarians, he sent an envoy to the king of Hungary in 1520 demanding tribute. In what seems an incredible act of folly, as well as a cruel violation of diplomatic conduct, the envoy was either killed — according to some sources — or sent back with his ears and nose clipped.

Why this was done is something of a mystery; one theory is that the Hungarian court was fed up with the constant loss of resources and population to Turkish slavers and raiders in the border regions, and took this means of showing it. But the country was absolutely unprepared for any kind of war, let alone one with the great Ottoman Empire. The furious sultan was now ready to bypass the border fortresses and head straight for Buda. His advisors, however, reminded him that it was necessary to take the southern fortresses first, so as not to leave enemy garrisons in his rear, and he agreed.

The First Stage

The Turks, accordingly, proceeded overland in the direction of Belgrade in June 1521, their plans a secret to no one. The Hungarian government and the papacy began scrambling ineptly to raise money and men to meet the Ottoman army. Pope Leo X, who had first rejoiced in the accession of Suleiman under the impression that he was a man of peace, now sent a sizeable sum of money to Hungary. Emperor Charles V was urged to send help, but he was embroiled with the insurrection of the followers of a former priest named Martin Luther. When the Turkish menace had first threatened the next-door neighbor of the Holy Roman Empire, Luther had proclaimed that "to fight against the Turks is to resist the Lord, who visits our sins with such rods." By the time the Turks drew closer to Germany, the statement was causing him much embarrassment and he seems to have changed his tune, but meanwhile the Lutheran members of the Diet of Worms in 1521 refused the emperor's request for help for Hungary.

Accordingly, in 1521 Belgrade fell to the Turks despite a heroic defense, with the royal army not even in the vicinity. A tax was hastily imposed in Hungary for the purpose of defense, but the money seems to have been embezzled, and the Turkish victories continued. Not only Szabács but other smaller frontier forts were captured; by the time the Turks turned back, the few strongholds that were left stood isolated in the midst of devastated areas, prey to attacks by the Turkish raiders who remained in the region. Suleiman now turned his attention to Rhodes, as we saw in the previous chapter, and it was 1526 before he was able to get on with the plans for his future Ottoman province of Hungary.

The previous year, King Francis I of France had been defeated and imprisoned by Emperor Charles at the Battle of Pavia. From his prison cell, the royal jailbird had smuggled an appeal to the sultan, hidden in his envoy's shoe, urging him to help free him by attacking his jailor before the Habsburgs became still more powerful. Suleiman answered in a pompous letter, kindly encouraging the French prisoner and assuring him that "night and day our horse is saddled and our sword girt on." The sultan was going to continue his attack on the West anyway, but the letter may have given him an added incentive: why not go on to Vienna after Buda?

The Bumbling Road to Mohács

During the five-year respite from major invasion that Hungary enjoyed from 1521 to 1526, she should have been able to pull herself together and mobilize for the next onslaught. Again, however, chronic ineptitude plagued all efforts at organization. Frequent changes in governmental personnel did not help, nor did erratic financial decisions that failed to bring in needed revenue. There seems to have been little real patriotism, and a native Hungarian claimant to the throne, who had the support of a powerful faction of the country, even looked for support to the Turks — thereby constituting a fifth column within the nation. Protestantism had begun to infect Hungary from the west, undermining loyalty to the Catholic monarch. Appeals to crusade were identified with the Catholic Church and therefore generally rejected by Protestants everywhere. Nevertheless, it was clear that only outside help could save the country, and Hungarian representatives were sent out to obtain it.

Emperor Charles V, desperately trying to cope with the Peasants' War (sparked by Luther's teachings) of 1524–1525, was not in a position to do much for Hungary, and when he did manage to send troops in 1526, they arrived two days too late because the Protestant members of the Diet of Speyer would not authorize them in time. The other countries of Europe, always with the exception of the Papal States, were also a washout. Pope Adrian VI had sent a large quantity of grain for the provisioning of the castles in the path of the Turks, but only a small part of it arrived at its destinations. The rest was intercepted by a rogue captain and his cronies who seized it, sold it, and spent the money on themselves.

The new pope, Clement VII, did everything he could to assist in the defense of Hungary, including renewing the papal alliance with Ached of Egypt, an inveterate enemy of the Turks. Clement also sent the accomplished diplomat Baron Burgio, who had lived in Hungary, as a special papal nuncio to the country in 1524. Burgio found the king and the government so incompetent that he proceeded to Poland to seek help from the king's uncle, King Sigismund. He found that country in similar political disarray and returned to Buda in August 1524, where he found conditions even worse, with the king sending him to his council and the council sending him back to the king, and no action at all being taken. Burgio sent for Cardinal-Legate Campeggio, who was in Vienna, and the two of them tried to talk some sense into the do-nothing Hungarian government. The only effective response came from Archbishop Tomori of Kalocsa, who himself commanded troops in the south of the country. The cardinal-legate financed three hundred papal troops at his own expense to assist Tomori (and also talked him out of resigning in despair at the hopeless situation).

The political chaos within the country grew worse throughout 1525. On February 27 of that year, the nineteen-year-old king spent a lavish amount of money on masks and costumes for a carnival celebration. One of his relatives, George of Brandenburg, wrote: "The court of the King is terribly poor, but I had a very good time at the carnival." Lajos himself dressed as Lucifer, complete with horns, hoofs, and tail. "*Que fuit contra Deum et contra omnes sanctos,*" says the source: "Which was a mockery of God and all His saints."

In January 1526 Burgio reported on reports of massive preparations by the Turks, while the spendthrift king now had no funds left even for his own food. "My intelligence cannot fail to depress your holiness," wrote Burgio to the pope, "but it is my duty to write truthfully." Thoroughly alarmed, Pope Clement called in the diplomatic corps of Rome in February and informed them that although troops could no longer be sent because of wintry conditions, money could. He also wrote directly to the rulers of Europe in the same vein. The Hungarian officials were moved to tears at the dedication of the papacy to their cause, but recovered from their brief descent into patriotism to return to infighting and mutual recriminations. Now even Burgio asked to be recalled in the spring of 1526; he could do no more for Hungary if it would not help itself. "The king," he wrote, "in spite of my remonstrances, has gone hunting as if we were living in the midst of profound peace."

The day after the king went off on his hunting trip, word came that the sultan had left Constantinople bound for Hungary. Burgio went after the king and managed to bring him back for deliberations with his clueless ministers. Only Archbishop Tomori seems to have had the necessary courage and steadfastness to face the Turks, and the Nuncio furnished him with an additional 1,700 men and some artillery for his fortress of Pétervárad on the southern Danube. The king was voted near-absolute powers, but nobody obeyed him and he continued to sleep until noon every day. The pope sent more money, and granted permission for the king to dispose of Church property in Hungary in order to raise more.

On July 28, 1526, Tomori's fortress fell to an assault led by the Grand Vizier Ibrahim, while the archbishop was on his way to its relief. The garrison, half of it made up of papal troops, died heroically. The sultan, who kept a diary, recorded that the grand vizier had 500 of the defenders beheaded and 300 taken into slavery. Now the traditional bloody sword was carried throughout the kingdom summoning Hungarians to the defense of their country. By default, since there were no competent leaders willing to take command, the king himself led the army of perhaps 30,000, many of them raised by the nuncio. He seems to have started out from Buda with about 5,000, with the rest arriving en route — most of these seem to have been non-Hungarian volunteers or mercenaries. They rode out to meet the Turks on the plain of Mohács, northwest of Belgrade.

The Fatal Battle

In the meantime, the Turks had been capturing towns and fortresses right and left, some of which surrendered voluntarily. It seems the Ottomans had expected this part of the campaign to take three months; it took instead three days. At Mohács, the Christian army came upon the Turks on August 29, as part of the enemy army was about to make camp, while others were still arriving. According to some sources, Archbishop Tomori realized that if an attack were made immediately the enemy would be caught off guard and there would be some hope of success. There was a delay, however, with the Hungarians first deciding to make camp also and starting to remove their armor. When Tomori's plan was adopted, they had to rearm and regroup, thus losing valuable time.

Once the attack was decided, the king took the lead, ordering all to call on Christ the Savior, and charged the enemy. Following up what seemed like an easy penetration of the Turkish lines, they came up against the Janissaries with the sultan himself in their midst. In the fierce hand-to-hand combat that followed, the sultan was in some danger, but it soon passed. The whole battle, in fact, was short as battles go; it lasted perhaps three hours, though some Turkish sources claim it went on until nightfall. Twenty thousand of the Hungarians were dead, including many nobles, five bishops, and two archbishops — one of them the heroic Tomori. The remnants fled, including King Lajos. As he was crossing a stream, his horse reared and he fell into the water and drowned, weighed down by his heavy armor. The sultan noted in his diary the following day that two thousand prisoners were massacred.

The Aftermath of Mohács

Thus began nearly two hundred years of oppression and internal division for Hungary. The country was not only occupied by the Turks but a prey to the religious divisions caused by the Reformation, and by an interminable political struggle over the throne. Since the widow of Lajos II was a Habsburg princess, the way was open for that family, in the person of the king's brother-in-law Archduke Ferdinand, to claim the throne of Hungary. A series of Hungarian candidates would make the same claim, often depending on the help of the sultans, who regarded them as useful puppets. The country was thus to be long divided in its allegiance, with two "kings" plus the Turks, in a tripartite system with the Ottomans largely calling the shots.

As for Suleiman, he proceeded to Buda. On September 4 he casually noted in his diary that he had had the peasants in the camp slaughtered except for the women. He also noted that the Turkish raiders were forbidden to take plunder, but as we have seen at Rhodes, he does not seem to have enforced such prohibitions. On September 10 he entered Buda. Having looked around and looted its treasures — including the great library and other collections of King Matyas Corvinus — he burned the city, and withdrew. The campaigning season was drawing to a close with the approach of winter, but he would be back, three years later. On their way out, of course, his army ravaged the countryside in the usual Turkish fashion, plundering, massacring thousands, taking large numbers into slavery, and generally leaving misery and havoc in their wake. They did not have it all their own way, however, as bands of loyal Hungarians harassed their rear guard, taking some prisoners and killing others.

Breakfast in Vienna

Suleiman's next Hungarian adventure began when he left his capital in May 1529. The Hungarian claimant to the throne, János Zapolya, came to greet his overlord on the very field of Mohács that had seen the demise of his country. He apparently also allowed himself to be crowned by Suleiman with the holy crown of St. Stephen. Buda, now defended by the army of Ferdinand, who had been elected king of Hungary by a pro-Habsburg faction, fell easily to the Turkish assault, and Suleiman pushed on to Vienna, which he began to attack on September 22. Because of another war that Emperor Charles V was fighting in Italy, Ferdinand had only about 12,000 men to defend the city against a force of what was reputed to be 250,000 Turks, though that is surely an inflated figure. It was in any case larger than the army at Mohács three years earlier; possibly the total approached 100,000.

Ferdinand resorted to conscription and frantic appeals to the many regions of the Habsburg Empire, as well as to the Diet of Speyer. Luther, now that the Turks were getting close to *him*, made a grudging appeal for a united front against the Turks, which allowed Protestants and Catholics together to vote for a troop levy. Thereafter, the Catholic Habsburgs were obliged to make concessions to the Protestants in order to buy their loyalty in the anti-Turkish struggle, while the Turks began to look more and more favorably on the Christian heretics as useful pawns.

Fortunately, heavy rains delayed the Turks while the Austrians mobilized, bringing the Vienna garrison up to 20,000 men. Drastic measures were taken, such as razing all structures outside the walls that could serve as shelter for the enemy; this meant some 800 buildings, including churches, convents, a hospital, and even a castle. The elderly, women, children, and priests were evacuated, though the advance Turkish raiders picked off many as they left the city. Suleiman had not brought his heavy artillery and so relied on mining operations. Meanwhile he demanded surrender from the defenders, claiming that he would be eating breakfast in their city within three days, and would then obliterate it and its inhabitants completely. Two weeks later, he was still waiting for that breakfast. The Austrians sent out a Turkish prisoner with a message to the sultan that his breakfast was getting cold; the Turks were getting cold too, as the chilly rains poured down on their light tents. And where the Turkish mines had made breaches, the defenders repulsed those who tried to enter and made some sorties of their own, bringing back prisoners and even camels.

Suleiman tried winning over the Viennese with sumptuous gifts sent in by released Christian prisoners, but nothing seemed to work for him. Finally, on October 12, his war council advised withdrawing due to the complaining of the troops and the approaching end of the fighting season. It was decided to make one more attempt on October 14, led by the Janissaries, with lavish rewards promised to those who would get into the city. It failed, and now the Turkish losses were so heavy and the men so discouraged that the sultan agreed to withdraw. All prisoners were massacred or burned alive, except for young men and women destined for slavery. The bells of St. Stephen's rang out the *Te Deum* and the Ottoman propaganda ministry had to come up with a face-saving story: the sultan had not really intended to take Vienna; he had merely come to confront the Emperor Charles, who was too cowardly to meet him.

Sometimes Suleiman did not know when to give up. In 1532 he came trudging wearily up the Danube again, still obsessed with Vienna. This time he could not even make it past the stubborn border fortress of Köszeg. Twelve separate assaults on the town and its fortifications were repulsed all through the month of August. The garrison inside exploded the Turkish mines harmlessly, while once more the Christian rain bedeviled the Turks. It was face-saving time again. The sultan magnanimously decided to pardon the defenders of Köszeg, in return for a purely paper surrender, after which the he could honorably withdraw. The Turks pillaged and massacred on their way out of Hungary as usual, but they also suffered casualties in encounters with Austrian troops.

Of course, being Suleiman, he would not leave things at that. In 1540 he set off again for Hungary. In the meantime, the two kings, Ferdinand Habsburg and János Zapolya, had divided the country between them, with the understanding that if Zapolya died without an heir — as seemed likely because of his age and poor health — Ferdinand would be the sole king. George Martinuzzi, however, an anti-Habsburg monk, had persuaded Zapolya to marry a Polish princess who bore him a child just before he died, to Suleiman's delight. So there were still two kings. Ferdinand was unable to take Turkish Buda, and in 1541 Suleiman was back in the country, which was gradually being transformed into a Turkish province, even as its churches were being transformed into mosques. In 1543 the sultan captured the episcopal city of Esztergom, seat of the primate of Hungary; many other towns, cities and fortresses fell, and soon the bulk of the country was within the Ottoman Empire. A further campaign by the Turkish army in 1552 conquered more pockets of resistance, but by no means all.

Turkish Hungary

Conditions in Hungary in the Turkish period were worse than the ones we have seen in the Balkans, because most of Hungary did not provide the refuges and inaccessible areas of the mountainous Balkan region. With few places in which to hide, the population formed an easy target for raiders and slave-traders. The slavers were particularly active in Hungary because for some reason Hungarians were highly valued in the slave markets of Constantinople. In the Balkans, the Orthodox Church had come to an accommodation with the Turkish authorities that was not possible to the still-devout Roman Catholic Hungarians. To dilute the Faith that sustained their stubborn resistance, the Turks favored the increasing number of Protestants, even arranging debates between the two religions in order to promote discord.

Each of the several Turkish campaigns in Hungary also brought its aftermath of burning, slaughter, and pillage, so that the intervals of peace were often brief. Because all the land belonged to the Ottoman state, a fifth of it — Allah's part — was under direct state administration and the rest turned over as fiefs to soldiers and officials. Since these were often stationed in the country only temporarily, they sucked their holdings dry before they left. In "Allah's part" there was often better management and even some autonomy for the inhabitants, but it was a matter of degree. The insecurity, poverty, malnutrition, slave raiding, and disease that racked much of the countryside actually obliterated from people's minds the memory of the prosperous towns that used to stand where now there was only a village or nothing at all.

Royal Hungary, the western and northern part under Habsburg control, was not immune to these ills, because the frontier fortresses that protected it were often taken by siege or at least unable to protect the areas around them. Austrian administration could also be harsh, and taxes were zealously collected to meet the needs of defense. Still, tax collectors cannot be everywhere, and in some areas there seems to have been little tight control by either Turks or Austrians. In those places, the population was able to live a somewhat normal life with minimal interference from the authorities. As for the fortresses that defied conquest, there were examples of noble courage, faith, and heroism connected with so many of them that it might almost be said that the true Hungarian spirit survived within their walls. We can only consider two of them here, the great fort of Eger, gateway to northern Hungary, and Szigetvár, which turned out to be death for Suleiman.

The Great Siege of Eger, 1552

The town and fortress of Eger are located to the northeast of Buda, south of a mining region around Kassa that furnished important revenues to the kingdom. It also barred the way to northern Hungary, in which Austrian troops were scarce. If the Turks broke through to the north, they would be able more easily to move again against Vienna. The fortress was large, with several bastions and gates, and good positions for cannon placement. In the spring of 1552, two large Turkish armies were moving toward Eger, encouraged by a series of victories elsewhere; they comprised about 80,000 soldiers and nearly as many logistical troops, craftsmen, and others who always accompanied the Ottoman armies. They also had some of the super-sized cannons the Turks had been using so effectively since the siege of Constantinople, numerous smaller pieces of artillery, and lots of camels and other animals. Eger to them looked like an easy target. The defenders — 2,000 at the most, including women — were outnumbered forty or fifty to one; despite frantic pleas to King Ferdinand and others, no assistance was sent during the entire siege of some thirty-four days in September and October 1552.

The commander of the fortress was István Dobó, an inspired leader of the dedicated and courageous defenders. One of his officers, Gergely Bornemissza, showed extraordinary inventiveness in the use of explosives: he made grenades, stuffed barrels with gunpowder and rolled them down on the besiegers, and even transformed a water-wheel by filling it with gunpowder and arranging its fuse in such a way that it did not merely explode but sent flames in all directions, creating multiple fires within the enemy's ranks as it rolled through them. Many of the residents of the town of Eger who had not fled crowded into the fortress, along with the wives and children of the garrison, and all helped in the cause. Children acted as pages and fetched supplies, while women tended the wounded and poured boiling lead, oil, or water onto the Turks attempting to climb the walls. Some of the women took up the swords of their fallen husbands and joined the combat. The several priests within the walls administered the sacraments, buried the dead, and fought on the walls with the rest.

Day after day the Turkish assaults were beaten back with great losses, until finally the Ottoman troops had to be forcibly driven forward by their officers; even the commanders of the two Turkish armies began to quarrel, and food became scarce. The defenders had not only adequate food, until the last couple of days, but they had cellars full of the legendary Bull's Blood wine of Eger, the Egri Bikavér. Until the last day they drank it watered by order of Commander Dobó, but during the final hours that decided the outcome, he is said to have ordered the best of the remaining wine, unwatered, brought out to cheer the fighters. It must have helped, as we shall soon see.

By the morning of that last day, the bastions and walls of the fortress were in ruins, numerous defenders were dead or wounded, and there were still masses of Turks left down below preparing to mount a final attack on the crumbling ramparts. Dobó assembled all those still alive and unfurled the banners of Our Lady, St. Stephen, and St. John. He had the priests expose the Blessed Sacrament, before which all knelt. The author of a famous novel about the siege, based on extensive research in contemporary documents, records — or imagines — a final speech by the Deputy Commander Mekcsey that includes the stirring words: "In the sacred elements we see here we know that the living Christ is present. He is with us!" All prayed aloud, and the priests gave general absolution. It was October 14.

By nightfall, after a hideous day of hand-to-hand combat in which both women and men were engaged, the enemy had once more been beaten back. The next morning requiem Mass was said for the three hundred dead within the fortress, bringing the total Christian losses to perhaps seven hundred; the Turks spent the next few days burying their eight thousand dead; how many thousands they had lost in their several other failed assaults is unknown. Their artillery continued to bombard the fort, though there was no assault on the disintegrating walls. Fall came early that year and there had already been cold rain during part of the siege, but now the Christian snow began. It was reported that the Janissaries had refused to return to the assault, and that Turks were slipping away from the camp even before receiving orders from the commanders. Soon the whole body of Turkish survivors was in headlong retreat. In their haste, they left their tents and much else that the battered defenders were later able to salvage.

In Rome, the Pope said a Mass of thanksgiving, and Christian Europe rejoiced in the stunning victory; Eger was to remain Hungarian for another four decades. In 1596, when the fortress was manned by mercenaries rather than regular soldiers, the Turks returned and easily captured it. They kept Eger for ninety-one years as one of their administrative centers, turning many churches into mosques, until it was finally liberated in the great crusade described in the following chapter.

Glory and Tragedy at Szigetvár, 1566

We recall that Suleiman, after the Turkish failure to take Malta, had remarked with exasperation that apparently if he wanted something done he had to do it himself, and had promised to go to Malta in the spring. By the spring of 1566, however, he had another project to dispose of: the stubborn Hungarian fortress of Szigetvár, northeast of Mohács, which ten years earlier had repelled an assault by the Pasha of Buda and caused the loss of several thousand Turkish troops. Here again, Suleiman reflected bitterly, was a case where he just had to do the thing himself. Though he had been ailing for some time and apparently also suffering from depression — possibly because of the death of his favorite wife, Roxelana, or his own physical decline — he determined to see to the capture of Szigetvár in person. In May, accordingly, he left the capital on his thirteenth campaign with perhaps the largest army he had yet led; it was his seventh foray into Hungary.

En route, the son of the pretender János Zapolya, now a young man, came groveling into the imperial presence and was kindly received by his overlord. The journey was hard on the aging Sultan. His tent was flooded and he had to squeeze in with the grand vizier, and he traveled in a curtained carriage because he could no longer ride for long periods. The convoy traveled faster than it was supposed to, irritating the exhausted sultan so much that he wanted to have the overzealous quartermaster beheaded. The vizier talked him out of it, and he contented himself with ordering the execution of the governor of Buda instead.

While the Magnificent was on his way, a man who hated everything he stood for was preparing to meet him. The pleas of the defenders of the fortress for help from the large Austrian army poised to bar the road to Vienna to the Turks had met with no response, so Miklos Zrinyi, viceroy of Croatia and veteran of the Turkish siege of Vienna, volunteered to take charge of the defense, and began by erecting a large cross within the fortress. With only 2,500 men against perhaps 90,000 approaching Turkish troops, it was obviously a hopeless situation. Nevertheless, Zrinyi was determined to sell his life and those of his comrades very dearly. He first managed to slay a local Turkish governor, which so enraged the sultan that he could hardly wait for his revenge. The siege began in early August and the town around the fortress was soon taken by the enemy and the women and children slain, but at a cost of 3,000 Turks killed to 300 Hungarians.

Within the fortress were the wives and daughters of the garrison officers, determined to share their fate. The Turks offered the commander two whole provinces to rule if only he would surrender, and sent messages on arrows into the fort attempting to persuade the soldiers to open the gates. Not surprisingly, none of the enemy's offers was accepted and the siege went on, with the defenders' artillery making large holes in the Turkish ranks.

August 29 was the anniversary of Mohács, and Suleiman undoubtedly remembered his victory of forty-five years earlier; he urged greater efforts, even as the defenders hoisted the black flag that meant they were prepared to die to the last man. September 5 saw a huge hole blown in the walls by a Turkish mine, signaling the approach of the end for the garrison. But the sultan died that night, still hoping in vain for news from the siege. His death was concealed until word could reach his successor, and the corpse was embalmed with the innards removed and buried, apparently in the Hungarian town now called Szulimán.

It took five more days for Szigetvár to fall. Dressed in his wedding suit, holding his father's jeweled sword and the flag, Zrinyi prepared his three hundred remaining men for death. As the Janissaries poured through the breech, the defenders' artillery killed hundreds of them. The commander and all but three of his men then perished, fighting to the death. As the Turks flocked into the ruins to search for a rumored treasure, a young woman who was still alive managed to set alight the gunpowder stored in the cellar. The explosion killed some three thousand more Turks, bringing their total losses to 25,000 men, to the defenders' 2,500. Because of the sultan's demise, the Turks withdrew, all the way back to Constantinople. It is hard to imagine there was much celebrating of their technical victory; Zrinyi had so clearly won.

After Suleiman

Throughout the rest of the sixteenth century and for most of the seventeenth, the political situation retained the same structure, though with changing players and shifting alliances. The Habsburg claimants to the Hungarian throne held varying amounts of northern and western Hungary. They were generally unable to make much progress against the Turks, to the bitter disappointment of their Hungarian supporters, because they were so hard-pressed by either the Protestants within their empire's borders or by external enemies — usually the kings of France. Some of these Habsburg rulers seem to have been heartily disliked by their Hungarian subjects, while others managed to win them over to some extent. The sphere of the "national" pretenders was centered on the southeast mountainous region of Transylvania, which had come to be a center of heresy as well. Sometimes the Transylvanian pretenders made agreements with the Habsburgs so that there was only one king; mostly, however, they allied with the Turks against the Habsburgs. They were often Protestant and prone to start rebellions.

The Seventeenth Century

In 1606, following several years of indecisive campaigns against the Turks by the Habsburgs, to which the papacy contributed both large sums of money and tens of thousands of troops, a peace treaty was signed that held throughout the first half of the seventeenth century. There were still border skirmishes, and some fortresses and towns within occupied Hungary still heroically resisted capture, but no major campaigns occurred. The peace with the Turks allowed for the development, in certain parts of the country, of the beginnings of a Catholic restoration that was desperately needed. The loss of so many of the upper clergy at Mohács, and destruction of churches and monastic communities during the Turkish wars had left the common people without shepherds and a prey to proselytizing wolves. At one point the land of St. Stephen seems to have become eighty to ninety percent Protestant. Some measures had been taken by Hungarian bishops to implement the reforms of the Council of Trent in the second half of the sixteenth century, and in the early seventeenth century a number of prominent Protestants became Catholic.

The reconversion of the country, promoted by major figures in the Hungarian Church such as Cardinal Peter Pázmány, himself a convert from Calvinism, was greatly assisted by the work of the Jesuits. They founded schools and colleges throughout Hungary, while Pázmány founded a Catholic university, and missionary work in Transylvania and in Ottoman Hungary began. Cardinal Pázmány also worked to obtain papal collaboration with the Habsburgs in an all-out campaign against the Ottomans and their allies during the 1630s, but in vain. (It will be recalled that this was the period of the Thirty Years' War, which absorbed the full attention of the European nations as well as the popes.) It would not be until the end of the century that the cardinal's hopes were realized. In the meantime, he did what he could to combat Islam by writing a critique of the *Qur'an* and its teachings.

The situation changed in the second half of the century. With the cessation of the Thirty Years' War, the states of Europe were more inclined to consider the ever-present Turkish threat, particularly since internal developments at the Ottoman court had led to a more aggressive foreign policy. Papal dissatisfaction with the ecclesiastical policies of Louis XIV late in the century led to more cordial relations between the papacy and the Habsburgs and a revival of the crusading spirit in Rome. Popes Alexander VII and Clement X supported the project of a new anti-Ottoman alliance, with both military and diplomatic means. We will see it unfold in the next chapter.

Main Works Consulted

Halecki, Oscar. *Borderlands of Western Civilization.*

Hegyi, Klára and Zimányi, Vera. *The Ottoman Empire in Europe.*

Kinross, Lord. *The Ottoman Empire.*

Komjathy, Anthony Tihamer. *A Thousand Years of the Hungarian Art of War.* Quotation on p. 39.

Macartney, C. A. M. *Hungary.*

Pastor, Ludwig von. *History of the Popes,* vols. VII and X. Quotations from papal diplomatic sources on pp. 176 and 177 of X.

Peres, Géza. *The Fall of the Medieval Kingdom of Hungary.*

Sinor, Denis. *History of Hungary.*

Sugar, Peter F., *et al. A History of Hungary.*

Zombori, István, *et al. A Thousand Years of Christianity in Hungary.*

Nine

The Anti-Jihad Victorious:
Lepanto to Vienna and After

The death of Suleiman, the last great Ottoman sultan, was a turning point for the West as well as the Muslim East, although this was not immediately apparent. Suleiman had filled key posts in his administration with highly competent men, including the Grand Vizier Sokollu who was still in office at his master's death. The continuation of efficient and effective government masked, for a while, the real disaster that struck the empire following the demise of Suleiman: its name was Selim.

Suleiman's Murders of His Sons and Grandsons

Suleiman had had two sons who might have made worthy successors: Mustafa, his favorite, probably the best suited to be sultan, and Bayazid. He also had a clever Slavic wife, Roxelana, a born Machiavellian, who acquired such influence over the sultan that she was able to manipulate affairs of state to suit her own ends, even arranging for the murder of the talented Grand Vizier Ibrahim, of whom she was jealous. Bayazid and Selim were her sons, while Mustafa was the son of another mother. Naturally Roxelana schemed to present him in a treasonous light to his father. Whatever the truth of the matter, Suleiman believed

the rumors of Mustafa's unfaithfulness and summoned him to
his presence. When the young man arrived, he was attacked by
a number of the mutes whom the Ottoman sultans were wont
to employ for such purposes; with his father egging them on,
they strangled him.

That left Bayazid and Selim. They had been at war with each
other even during Suleiman's lifetime, and Bayazid and his four
young sons were forced to take refuge with the shah of Persia.
In Suleiman's eyes this was treason too. Under great pressure,
the shah reluctantly allowed Ottoman executioners to enter his
country; they strangled Bayazid, ignoring his plea to be allowed
first to embrace his sons. The boys were strangled also, but there
was still a three-year-old son in another city. His grandfather
Suleiman sent a servant to strangle him too. The Lawgiver was a
law unto himself. Now it was clear that his surviving son Selim
would be the next sultan.

Selim the Drunkard

Selim II, the Sot, was a disaster for the empire in every way.
He didn't even look like an Ottoman sultan, with his red face
and short, fat body; whispers spread that he might really be an
illegitimate son of Roxelana — though he showed no signs of
her intelligence and cleverness. He was so addicted to wine that
he wrote poetry to it and repealed the laws against buying or
drinking it. An obsequious chief cleric thereupon declared that
since the sultan drank wine, it was permitted to the subjects.
(Never mind the *Qur'an*.) The Sot inherited an empire of 40,000
square miles, an undefeated fleet, and the Ottoman dream of
being sole emperor of the world, though he did nothing on
his own initiative to make that dream come true. While Selim

frittered away his life in debauchery, Grand Vizier Sokollu continued Suleiman's policies. In 1568 he negotiated an eight-year peace with the Holy Roman Empire while he dealt with Russian advances to the northeast and thought up a plan to link the Don and Volga rivers by a canal. The Muslim Khan of the Crimea, however, was able to persuade the Turkish troops sent into his territory that the north was really no place for Muslims: nights were often so short that a believer had no sooner finished evening prayers than it was time for the morning ones, and it was very cold in the north. Enthusiasm within the army for moving further north waned, Sokollu's plans fizzled, and a long-lasting peace broke out between sultan and tsar. Another plan spawned by Sokollu's fertile brain, a canal at Suez, also came to naught and the grand vizier turned his thoughts in yet another direction — westward.

The Mediterranean Again

At Tunis, the ruler installed by Charles V had been driven out by the Ottoman governor of Algiers, although the Spanish continued to hold the citadel. Within Spain itself, the Moorish community that had remained in the country after the capture of Granada in 1492 had begun a serious rebellion in 1567; it spilled over the borders of Granada and resulted in the desecration and destruction of churches and the torture and slaughter of many civilians. These Moors were reinforced by Muslims from Algiers, and appealed to the Sultan in Constantinople for more aid. Sokollu was receptive; he saw Spain as the Turks' main Mediterranean enemy, which he hoped to defeat with French help. Selim, however, was opposed. A very different target had attracted his capricious attention.

Although the Ottoman Empire was at peace, as usual, with the Venetians, Selim knew that Venice had taken over the island of Cyprus and that Cyprus produced excellent wine. It did not take much urging on the part of a couple of royal favorites, who hoped for valuable plunder from the island, to persuade him to order an attack upon it. It was the only time he overruled Sokollu, who had no choice but to comply. While the Catholics of southern Spain formed militias and successfully beat back the Moorish attacks in Granada — due largely to the leadership of twenty-two-year-old Don Juan of Austria, half-brother of King Phillip II — the Sultan was sending a list of grievances to Venice and demanding either satisfaction for supposed offenses or the ceding of the island of Cyprus to him. The Venetians naturally refused, and the fleet that the grand vizier had thought would sail to Spain sailed against Cyprus instead. The year was 1570, and Cyprus was the last significant Christian bastion in the eastern sea.

Atrocities on Cyprus

The Turkish army of about 50,000 men sent to Cyprus was under the command of Selim's favorite tutor, Lala Mustafa, who was also a rival of Sokollu. Piali Pasha, who had been at the siege of Malta, commanded the fleet. On the island, the Catholic Venetians had apparently established an oppressive feudal regime much resented by the Orthodox peasants, and tens of thousands of them were thought to be willing to join the Turks when they landed. The Venetians proceeded to kill 400 Cypriots suspected of planning an uprising, which added to the hostility against Venice. Upon arrival, the Turks treated the natives well and promised a period of tax exemption if they were victorious. Still, the people do not seem to have actively joined the Turkish attack on the Venetians, although they furnished supplies and information to the Ottoman army. Of the two Venetian cities Nicosia, the capital, surrendered after a six-week siege, but the Turks did not honor the terms of the capitulation; the remaining defenders and thousands of civilians were massacred, the city sacked, and the cathedral turned into a mosque. Several hundred enslaved women and boys were loaded onto a ship bound for Constantinople. One of the women was Amalda de Rocas who, before the ship got underway, managed to blow it up, killing those aboard but saving them from a terrible fate. Now it was the turn of the other city.

The Fate of Famagusta

Throughout the attack on the island, the European powers had been aware of events and the pope, in particular, had ceaselessly tried to rally support for the beleaguered defenders. It appears that a relief fleet had actually been assembled, but disagreements among the commanders and reluctance on the part of Admiral Doria, commanding the Spanish contingent, to risk his ships against the Turks prevented an effective attack on the enemy. The fleet returned to Italy, losing several ships to a storm on the way. Famagusta was left to its fate.

Lala Mustafa had expected the city to crumple under assault as easily as Nicosia had, but three months into the siege the Turks were still not within the walls. He wrote to the sultan that the place was not defended by men but by giants. The giants, however, together with their wives and children and the whole civilian population, were beginning to starve. Low on ammunition, they recovered unexploded Turkish mines and used the powder in them; they also kept a fire burning in a ditch outside the walls, using a smelly type of wood that the Turks could not stand. At last General Bragadino agreed to surrender, and Mustafa promised to spare all the inhabitants of the city and allow them to leave the island. Turkish ships would transport the surviving soldiers to Crete.

Again, a city driven to surrender trusted to the promises of the Turkish besiegers that the inhabitants would be spared, and again the enemy refused to honor its own terms. When Bragadino met with the Ottoman general on August 4, 1571 to deliver the keys of the city, what apparently began as an amicable meeting turned sour with, first, the accusation that the Venetian commander had massacred Turkish prisoners, and secondly, that he should give hostages — here Mustafa seems to have indicated one of Bragadino's pages, at whom he had been leering — for the safe return of the Turkish ships that would transport the survivors. This Bragadino refused as being contrary to the surrender agreement. Selim's tutor then flew into a maniacal rage, to which it seems he was prone, and repudiated the capitulation agreement. The Venetians who had come with their general were hacked to pieces, the young pages taken off in chains. Mustafa is said to have personally cut off Bragadino's nose and ears before imprisoning and subjecting him to various humiliations, such as being led around the Turkish camp on all fours. Finally, he was summoned to convert to Islam and refused. He was thereupon slowly flayed alive; he could be heard whispering prayers until he finally expired, to all appearances a martyr of the Faith. His skin was stuffed and paraded around before being flown from Lala Mustafa's flagship. Most of the prisoners and residents of the city were massacred.

Pope St. Pius V Sounds the Alarm

The West had not gone to the defense of Cyprus, but at least one man had seen the danger of further Turkish aggression with great clarity. In 1570, Pope St. Pius V was already contacting the chief rulers of the West to urge them to unite against an enemy that threatened them all. Unstable Charles IX of France, the longtime ally of the Turks, was one of a series of sickly sons of the opportunistic queen mother, Marie de Medici. He was not interested in a crusade, and certainly Queen Elizabeth of England, also an ally of the Turks, was not. Even Philip II of Spain, champion of the Catholic cause against the Protestants, was much occupied with his new American empire and other affairs and did not answer the papal summons in person. He did, however, send his young half-brother, Don Juan of Austria, as well as dozens of ships. Holy priests and monks, many of them the Jesuits of St. Francis Borgia, general of the order, to whom the pope had confided his hopes for the crusade, crisscrossed the continent preaching and seeking volunteers, prayer, and sacrifice for the cause.

By mid-1571, the Papal States, Spain, and (after some prickly negotiations) Venice had formed a Holy League for concerted action against the Ottoman fleet. They were joined by virtually all the Catholic maritime powers, including Genoa, Savoy, Urbino, Tuscany and, of course, the Knights of Malta. The Knights had recently lost a number of their ships and were able to send only three; still, three ships manned by the Maltese Knights was probably equal to twice that number of other vessels. Don Juan, the pope's choice for commander, managed to assemble 208 ships (some eighty fewer than the Turks had).

On the flagship of the Genoese admiral, Giovanni Andrea Doria, was a curious picture that Philip II of Spain had sent him. Philip had received it from the archbishop of Mexico, who had commissioned it as a copy of the mysterious image of Mary that had appeared in 1531 on the cloak of an Aztec Indian. The archbishop, hearing the news from Europe of the Turkish offensives and the scramble to organize an effective defense, must have thought of the many miracles already associated with the image of Our Lady of Guadalupe. When the copy was finished, he touched it to the original and sent it to the king, advising him to have it displayed on one of the ships of the Holy League, in the hope of victory. Pope St. Pius was also seeking Our Lady's aid through the recitation of the Rosary, which he asked all of Europe to pray for a successful outcome of the Christian offensive. When the ships set out from the Sicilian port of Messina on September 16, 1571, with the banner of Christ Crucified flying from the flagship of Don Juan, all of the men had rosaries too.

They headed first for the island of Corfu, reaching it on September 27 or 28. There they received a shock: the Turks had been there and gone, leaving a ghastly ruin behind them. Churches and houses were destroyed, and the bodies of men, women, and children lay strewn about, the prey of vultures. Defiled and mutilated crucifixes gave evidence of the Turks' hatred for Christianity. While the fleet was at Corfu, Don Juan's scouts reported on the location of the Turkish fleet and the Christian armada headed there. Soon after came a report came of the atrocities at Famagusta: now the crusaders, especially two of Bragadino's brothers who were ship commanders, were galvanized with the desire to avenge the Christian dead of Corfu and Cyprus.

The Battle of Lepanto

In Rome, on October 5, Pope Pius had been meeting with his treasurer. Suddenly he rose, went to the window, and stood gazing intently at the sky. Then, turning, he said, "This is not a moment for business; make haste to thank God, because our fleet this moment has won a victory over the Turks." What the pope apparently saw in vision — for the news could not possibly have reached him by natural means — was a battle occurring at that very moment which has been called the greatest sea battle since the Battle of Actium in 31 B.C., when the forces of Mark Antony and Cleopatra fought the fleet of Octavian (the future Caesar Augustus).

On the Christian fleet, very early on October 7, Mass had been said and general absolution given, and priests were moving around each ship encouraging the men. Don Juan had ordered the rowers — often criminals or prisoners of war — to be loosed from their chains and armed; he promised them freedom if they fought well. The Turkish fleet was anchored in the Gulf of Lepanto, near Corinth, as the allied fleet approached. The Turkish ships outnumbered the Christians', but the number of combatants seems to have been about equal, perhaps 30,000 on each side. The Christians had the considerable advantage of possessing six galleasses; these were larger than galleys and had side-mounted cannon — as opposed to the front-mounted cannons of the galleys. This allowed them to inflict great damage on any ship that came broadside to them.

Some accounts say that as the fleets came within fighting distance of each other, early in the morning of October 7, the wind first favored the Turks and blew their ships forward against the

Christian vessels. But then the wind shifted, and Don John's ships were able to draw close to the enemy. Sixteenth-century naval warfare included hand-to-hand fighting on the decks as well as bombardment by cannons and arrows, and the Christian victory at Lepanto would be dearly bought. A woman known only as Maria the Dancer, dressed as a man, led the charge onto the deck of the Turkish flagship. By the late afternoon of October 7, when all was over, the sea was red with blood for miles around the battle site. The Holy League lost about 8,000 men and at least double that number wounded, but only a dozen ships. Around the same number of Turks died, but thousands more were captured; forty or fifty ships were sunk, and over a hundred were captured. The rest of the vessels — perhaps only a dozen, perhaps as many as forty — escaped back to Constantinople under the command of one of the admirals, Uluj Ali; he had fought at the siege of Malta, been defeated and survived. Now he had been defeated again, but as a consolation prize he brought with him the flag of the Knights of Malta, which he had captured. (The Christians had a bigger prize: the venerated banner of the Turks that came from Mecca and bore the name of Allah embroidered on it 28,900 times.)

An unforeseen development was the rising up, from the depths of the Turkish galleys, of several thousand Christian slaves who had been forced to row the enemy ships. Chesterton, in his great poem *Lepanto*, describes

> Thronging of the thousands up that labour under sea
> White for bliss and blind for sun and stunned for liberty.
> *Vivat Hispania!*
> *Domino Gloria!*
> Don John of Austria
> Has set his people free.

When the news reached Europe on October 21, there was general relief, rejoicing, and thanksgiving. Pope Pius V gave credit where it was due, declaring October 7 the Feast of Our Lady of Victory; it was later changed to the Feast of Our Lady of the Rosary — a name it still bears. When he received Don Juan, he quoted from St. John's Gospel, "There was a man sent from God whose name was John." In Constantinople, Sultan Selim actually fasted and prayed for three days, in his shock and dismay, and then wanted to have all the Spaniards and Venetians in his empire killed. Sokollu talked him out of it, and he subsided into his ordinary way of life.

Lepanto's Consequences

The significance of this great battle, the climax of the long Christian resistance to Muslim conquest by sea, was that it was the first major defeat of the Ottoman fleet. For it did not stop Turkish incursions; indeed, only six months after the battle a new fleet of over two hundred ships — including galleasses, this time — appeared first off Cyprus and then off Crete, though without making any moves to attack. The sight of it appalled and dismayed those who had written off the Turkish fleet: for although the naval power of the West was still superior, it was fragmented and hard to unify. No wonder the Venetians began to scramble for a new peace with the Turks, even at the cost of ceding Cyprus. As Sokollu remarked to the Venetian ambassador, "There is a wide difference between your loss and ours. In capturing Cyprus from you we have cut off one of your arms; in defeating our fleet you have merely shaved off our beard; the lopped arm will not grow again, but the shorn beard will grow stronger than before."

The year after Lepanto Don Juan re-conquered Tunis, but the year after that the Turks took it back again, this time permanently. In 1578 they extended their influence to Morocco and won a battle in which the Portuguese king was killed. Decidedly they were not finished yet. And the members of the Holy League, which France was again working to destroy, were already engaged in their mutual rivalries as if they had forgotten all about the Turks. No, victory at Lepanto didn't save Christendom with one stroke; the great thing was rather that the Ottoman Empire was no longer seen as invincible.

During the last decades of the sixteenth century there was also a change within the Ottoman Empire itself. Selim died suddenly after one last binge in 1574. His successor, Murad III, after having his five brothers strangled, proceeded to pursue his own vices of obsessive greed and lust, and also to get in Sokollu's way at every opportunity. The empire's army became bogged down in central Asian adventures that proved hard to resolve, and Sokollu's experience and good judgment were no longer wanted. With his assassination in 1579 the long decline of the Ottoman Empire was well underway, and would never be effectively reversed. Providence works in other ways than naval victories.

The Seventeenth Century

At the dawn of the 1600s, Europe's powers seemed in no shape to deal with the Turks. Spain was reeling from the defeat and destruction of the great fleet that Phillip II had sent against Queen Elizabeth's England in 1588, and would exhaust its remaining resources in the course of the Thirty Years' War from 1618–1648. Elizabeth had amicable commercial relations with the Ottomans and could not be counted on to support any new

European enterprise against them. In the mid-seventeenth century, England was wracked by the religious war that brought the dictator Oliver Cromwell to power. He was too busy trying to exterminate the Irish and puritanize England to think of fighting the Turks, while the kings who succeeded him had major problems of their own to deal with. France, whether controlled early in the century by the sinister Cardinal Richelieu in the reign of Louis XIII, or by the pompous and licentious Louis XIV, "the Sun King," for the rest of the century, pursued the shameful pro-Turkish policy that so ill befitted a Catholic state. The Holy Roman Empire was wracked in mid-century by the physical, religious, and political consequences of the Thirty Years' War. The Reformation, now a political as well as religious revolt against Catholicism, had seeped all over the continent, poisoning international relations and much else. What was going on in Hungary for most of this period we have seen in the previous chapter.

And then there was one unexpected development, which must have stunned the papacy and the other Catholic states committed to the defense of Europe: Venice changed sides again, this time wholeheartedly.

The War of Candia: 1645–1669

In 1645 the great island of Crete, then known by the name of its capital, Candia, was a Greek possession of Venice — and the last significant one — until the republic's Ottoman "allies" sent a fleet to capture it. The pretext was supposedly the capture by Maltese corsairs of a Turkish convoy bound for Egypt carrying valuable cargo, as well as a prominent lady of the harem and a royal baby. The incompetent and foolish Sultan Ibrahim flew into a rage and had to be persuaded not to massacre all the Christians in the empire; he merely imprisoned all the diplomats and closed down Christian businesses instead, but he still wanted more revenge. Someone remarked that the Knights of Malta were now mostly French, so he considered attacking France. From this too he was hastily dissuaded, and the grand vizier was able to substitute Crete for France by explaining that the Maltese squadron had anchored there. Venice was unprepared militarily, and the Thirty Years' War was absorbing the attention and resources of most of Europe. Still, in spite of the fact that Venice had consistently refused to help other Christians attacked by the Turks, the papacy, Spain, Tuscany, and the Knights of St. John scraped together a small fleet to support the Venetians.

It arrived too late, and Venetian diplomacy was unable to secure more assistance. (Now the Venetians knew how other Christians beleaguered by the Turks had felt.) But Crete was a large and valuable piece of real estate, and Venice would not give up the fight for it. By stringent financial measures it built a larger fleet and took the fight into Turkish territory, capturing a Dalmatian port in 1648 and winning many sea battles. In 1656 Venetians fought the Ottomans in a great battle at the very straits leading to Constantinople; they nearly reached the city itself in the following year, but were repulsed by the guns along the coast.

After twelve years, Venice was still pouring money, men, and resources into the war effort, although the Turks had begun to gain ground and the Venetians had lost naval superiority. And still the capital of Crete, Candia, held out. In the course of the war, that Ottoman baby captured in 1645 had grown up and become a priest, Father Osman. There may have been a scheme to use him as a bargaining chip by proposing him as a pretender to the throne of Mehmed IV. He seems to have dreamed of forming a new state that would somehow combine the features of both Byzantium and the Ottoman Empire, replacing them both, which of course appealed to almost nobody. Pope Clement IX worked desperately to obtain help for Venice, and finally extracted a small force from France, which fought under the papal flag so as not to irritate the Turks, and soon abandoned Candia. In 1669, the city was at last evacuated after twenty-three years of siege, in which as many as a hundred thousand men had died. The experience completely reversed both the Venetian position of trade supremacy, which she had lost to other countries while absorbed in the War of Candia, and her anti-papal and anti-Habsburg policy. Now Venice was a Catholic crusading state allied with the Habsburgs; the Jesuits who had been expelled from the city were allowed back. Now too, Venetians began to trade more by land and less by sea. It was safer.

The Mustafa Disaster

Despite the "conversion" of Venice to the anti-Turkish side, however, one would not have expected such a century to produce the most spectacular and decisive victories over the Ottoman Turks that had yet occurred; yet so it was to happen. It was due in large part to an outstanding pope, Innocent XI, whose reign from 1676 to 1689 was dedicated to enforcing orthodoxy and morality, and also to the formation of a new European union against the Ottomans. He would be a key figure in the successful resistance to the last great Turkish onslaught of 1683.

Western success would also come courtesy of the colossal blunders of a new grand vizier. In 1676, following Turkish campaigns in Poland, Ukraine, and other northern territories, the highly competent Grand Vizier Köprülü died prematurely of an illness to which the guzzling of large quantities of wine and brandy had contributed. Sultan Mehmed IV made a disastrous choice (though it was just the kind of thing you would expect from this sultan) in replacing him with Kara Mustafa.

As a minor, Sultan Mehmed had needed someone to run the state because he was too young; when he grew up, he needed someone to run the state because he was far more interested in hunting and collecting falcons and dogs than in managing his realm. He could not be persuaded to give up the chase and turn his attention to important affairs; periodically he promised to do so, but always broke his promise and took off for the hunting field once again. (He was eventually imprisoned and deposed by his exasperated subjects.) Thus Kara Mustafa wielded even more power than was usual for the holder of the great office of grand vizier.

He did his job conscientiously, promoting order and prosperity within the empire, but his real desire was for military fame and glory. The dark-complexioned "Black Mustafa" burned with pride and overpowering ambition, and his ostentatious lifestyle — thousands of harem inmates, slaves, eunuchs, dogs, horses, falcons — shocked even the royal court. To pay for it all he sold things: government offices, concessions to foreign diplomats, audiences with the sultan — and anything else for which he could extort money. He was violently anti-Christian and is said to have bragged that after he took Vienna he would stable his horses in St. Peter's Cathedral and then go off to fight Louis XIV. He lived big, thought big, and talked big, and the simple-minded sultan liked him. Yearning for glory, he trotted along on military campaigns or led them himself, unlike earlier viziers, and his failures against Russia and other enemies did not discourage him. Then he saw a new opportunity.

The Hungarian Protestant Revolt

The Turks, who had been unsuccessful in their attacks on Ukraine, began to follow the career of the Hungarian loose cannon named Imre Thököly, a zealous Calvinist who was twenty-two years old when he began a revolt to drive the Austrians out of northern Hungary in the late 1670s. When papal diplomacy succeeded in forging the Hungarian-Habsburg reconciliation mentioned in chapter nine, Thököly decided to turn to the Turks for help, and was welcomed with open arms. The pasha of Buda received him royally in 1682, and soon a joint army of Turks and rebels was off to conquer the whole country. They had great success, and Mehmed IV gave the traitor the title of King of Hungary and Croatia — as a vassal, of course, of the sultan.

The residents of the areas newly conquered by Thököly and his Turkish pals found the occupiers far worse than the Austrian army they replaced. Both the Turks and Thököly's men burnt, enslaved, and ruined, and the embattled Emperor Leopold was forced to agree to a truce in late 1682 to gain time to build up his defensive coalition. The rebels appealed to the Ottomans for more help against the Catholic Habsburgs, and the Turks prepared a large military force ready to move into Hungary. Louis XIV had already been supporting the Protestant rebels and assured the Turks of French neutrality in the case of war, which greatly encouraged Kara Mustafa in his plans for a large-scale assault on Europe.[6]

---

[6] It is certainly hard to see any justification for this treason to Catholic Europe on the part of a Catholic king. Perhaps his attachment to such policies was one of the elements that kept him from complying with the request of Our Lord, through St. Margaret Mary, for the consecration of himself and his realm to the Sacred Heart. No king who practiced devotion to the Sacred Heart could simultaneously collaborate with the enemies of Christianity.

Meanwhile, Pope Innocent XI was sending papal nuncios all over Europe to promote the Catholic cause and neutralize the French threat to Austria, the leading crusader power. As usual, it wasn't easy. The tangle of delicate negotiations, intercepted messages, and hard bargaining resulted in many frustrations, while the French sought to undermine any union against the Turks and worked to prevent Poland from joining the war effort. Only at the last minute, as the Turkish army was already on the move, was the pope able to secure the support of Poland, but only after a difficult all-night session of the Polish Diet. It would prove vital in the crucial battle. The papal nuncio wrote on Easter Sunday, April 18, 1683, "Last night the Diet came to an end, and thus the league and war against the Turks are accomplished facts. This is an extraordinary favor granted by God to Christendom in answer to your Holiness' prayers and supplications. It must be openly acknowledged that this is not the work of men, for no exertion, no eloquence and no diplomatic skill could have brought it about." The Holy League now consisted of the Holy Roman Empire, Venice, and Poland, and would later include Russia.

The pope had spent Lent in prayer and penance for the cause. He proclaimed jubilees and indulgences in order to bring about peace within quarrelsome Europe, and ordered the Prayer against Infidels to be said at Mass, as well as other public prayers. The previous year, the Venetian ambassador to Constantinople had reported that Pope Innocent was greatly respected by the Turks, who realized that he alone had the power to unite Christendom against them; indeed, he was the only obstacle to their plans that they feared.

The tricky enterprise of collecting funds for a war chest had been underway for a couple of years before the war began. The pope was generous to the poor and to victims of the Turks in the

Balkans and elsewhere, but strict with the financial resources of the Papal States. Those had to be carefully managed so that the maximum amount could be given to the war effort; the clergy and ecclesiastical properties were assessed an extra tax, and even the treasures of some churches were taken to help finance the cause. Voluntary gifts from the higher clergy, wealthy individuals, Portugal, many Italian cities, and other states added to the total. As the Turks approached, the West was as ready as it could be.

Kara Mustafa's Not-So-Glorious Campaign

The Ottoman army started out with music and enthusiasm. Not only was Kara Mustafa there, but the sultan had decided to come along too, with his whole harem. It was he who led the troops as far as Belgrade in early May of 1683, where they paused to await more troops coming from Asia, Wallachia, and Moldavia. Kara Mustafa led the forces on from there. Estimates of the total number of troops vary widely: Kara Mustafa and an Austria diplomat said 160,000, not counting the enormous supply train and personnel connected with it — nor the harem, presumably. Other figures have ranged from 90,000 to 200,000. Whatever the number, it was certainly the strongest Turkish attack on Europe since the first siege of Vienna in the previous century. The emperor had at first only 30,000, under Duke Charles of Lorraine, which prevented him from going on the offensive.

Once the Ottomans reached Hungary, the army of another Calvinist traitor from Transylvania, Prince Apafi, joined the Turkish forces while Thököly attacked in western Slovakia. Charles was forced to retreat toward Vienna as the fortresses on which he had counted for refuge fell to the enemy, and he feared being cut off. On July 7, he suffered an attack by the

Tartar allies of the Turks. Rumor exaggerated the damage done by the Asian nomads, and panic in Vienna sparked a general exodus that included the emperor and the diplomatic corps. Kara Mustafa was first supposed to capture two Hungarian border fortresses, those being the ostensible target of the expedition, but his eagerness for military glory caused him to neglect these targets and move directly on Vienna, saying that if he took that city "all the Christians would obey the Ottomans." A commander, Ibrahim Pasha, warned him that he should postpone taking Vienna until he had subdued the frontier region with its fortresses, but Mustafa sneeringly replied that the Pasha was an old man with a defective mind. He did pause on July 8, however, to massacre the garrisons of two forts and burn most of the stored grain.

Mustafa Before Vienna

As the huge army approached Vienna, the city's defense preparations were still incomplete. Had the Turks moved faster, they might have taken the city by storm, but their march was slow and they took days to surround the city and set up camp. The tens of thousands of tents, carts, and animals — including buffaloes and camels — must have been a daunting sight for the twelve thousand defenders to contemplate. The traditional arrow was shot into the city bearing a message that demanded its surrender and conversion to Islam, and offering safe conduct to the inhabitants in case they simply wished to surrender and leave. The leader of the defense, Count Starhemberg, sent no reply, and so the siege commenced. The defenders had a number of highly experienced and competent men in charge; one of them, the bishop of Wiener-Neustadt who was also Count Kolonitsch, had been a Knight of Malta and fought the Turks at Candia.

Oddly enough, the Turks had not brought their heaviest artillery, which may indicate that Kara Mustafa's pretense of only attacking border fortresses had extended to the guns he had brought; the presence of heavy cannon at a small-scale siege of a couple of fortresses would have given away his real plans. Out-gunned by the Viennese, the Turks began to mine the walls; but this wasn't begun until July 20, which was much too late since it allowed time for the entire civilian population to be mobilized along with the 10,000 troops of the Duke of Lorraine. Then the not-so grand vizier blundered again: relying on a defective plan of the fortifications made by an engineer of whom he thought highly (an apostate Capuchin, it was said). Misled, Mustafa directed his main assault on what turned out to be the strongest points in the city's fortifications. Naturally he made little progress, but he persisted, meanwhile sending a barrage of poisoned arrows and other missiles against the defenders. By August 12 the Turks had partially penetrated the fortifications and were parked stubbornly in front of the strongest bastion, the Burg. In the meantime, the defenders had begun to suffer from severe dysentery, as well as a shortage of manpower, and urgent messages were sent to the Duke of Lorraine, who had been occupied with defeating Thököly and trying to link up with the relief forces on the way from Austria and Poland; at night distress flares were sent up from the tower of St. Stephen's Cathedral.

By September 3 Mustafa had given up on the Burg bastion and evacuated its besiegers. The following day a huge mine made a breach in part of it, but the defenders were able to keep the Turks from getting through. The long delay in taking the city was demoralizing the Turks, many of whom had already scooped up enough booty earlier in the campaign and now only wanted to go home. Kara Mustafa seems to have made two more mistakes at this point: he hesitated to attack the city with full strength because, according to one Turkish historian, he was afraid the soldiers would get all the booty; he also ignored reports that a large Christian army was on the way to the relief of Vienna.

On September 10 and 11, as the defenders were nearing the end of their strength, rockets went up outside the city to signal the arrival of the relieving army of around seventy thousand, led by Polish King Jan Sobieski and Prince Charles of Lorraine. It might have been stopped at the Danube, and Kara Mustafa had supposedly ordered his Tatar allies to do this, but for some reason — perhaps dislike of him — they did not comply. In any case it was another major mistake on his part not to do the job himself. He had also failed to fortify the Kahlenberg hills over which the army came.

On September 12, the famous preacher Father Marco d'Aviano celebrated Mass with King Sobieski as his server. The priest then stood in view of the whole army holding up a crucifix and praying for victory. The relief army enthusiastically attacked the Turks, and once again Mustafa muffed it. He ignored advice to use the disciplined and well-trained Janissary units and relied instead on an inadequate cavalry. The Turks then broke and fled, leaving at least ten thousand dead behind them, as well as their entire camp and booty, including thousands of oxen, buffaloes, camels, and sheep. Sobieski wrote that the luxurious tents of the grand vizier included "baths, gardens, fountains, rabbit hutches, and a parrot." It seems that before retreating the Turks had killed all their Christian prisoners except for five hundred children, who were liberated by the victorious allies. Sobieski sent a message to the pope, paraphrasing Julius Caesar: "I came, I saw, God conquered." Kara Mustafa, on the other hand, had not conquered, and his future was ominous.

As one after the other of the Turkish-held fortresses in Hungary fell to the advancing allied troops, Kara Mustafa eventually got control of his panicked troops but was unable to make a stand. He retreated to Belgrade, intending to winter there and return to the charge in the spring. By now he had many enemies, however, and two of the higher-ranking ones persuaded the sultan to order his execution. The sultan complained that Mustafa had not asked his permission to attack Vienna, and was therefore responsible for the debacle. Mustafa was strangled in Belgrade on Christmas Day, 1683.

Still, inept as he had been, he may have been the only leader with the ability to organize a new campaign of revenge against the enemy; as it happened, his successors as grand viziers were even worse than he was.

Christendom Rejoices

While the Turks had been storming Vienna, the Catholics of Europe had been storming Heaven with prayers for their defeat. The pope wrote Sobieski that he was praying night and day; he had full confidence that the prayers would be answered, and would say, pointing to the crucifix, "The Lord will protect us." When the tremendous news came to Rome, there was great rejoicing and a solemn *Te Deum* sung at St. Mary Major, but also Requiem Masses for the some five thousand Christians who had fallen in the battle. The Turkish banner was taken to St. Peter's, but is today lost — reported to have been seized by the French at some point, perhaps during the occupation of the Papal States by Napoleon. The pope was hailed as the savior of Christendom for his organization of the victorious alliance despite many obstacles, but he himself gave the credit to the Blessed Virgin Mary, in whose honor he instituted the Feast of the Most Holy Name of Mary, now celebrated on September 12, the date of the great triumph over the Turks.

Elated, Pope Innocent dreamed of a complete conquest of the Ottoman Empire and its division among the Christian powers. Still hoping to win over Louis XIV, whom he still regarded as possessing at least some Christian sentiments, he proposed that if French naval power were used successfully against the Turks, Louis could become the new emperor of Byzantium. The French king, however, with his designs on the Holy Roman Empire, had been glad to see the Turks besieging Vienna; he had even attacked the Spanish Netherlands (a Habsburg possession) as the Turks were nearing the city. A crusader he certainly was not, and he probably would have made a lousy Byzantine emperor too.

After Vienna

The relief of Vienna was the beginning of a rapid rollback of the Turkish occupation forces, by a new Holy League that in 1684 included Venice, and the galleys of the pope, the Knights of Malta, and Tuscany. There was more trouble with the French, who attacked Genoa and continued to wreak havoc in the Netherlands and Luxemburg, despite the pope's impassioned letter to the king insisting that God Himself willed the war against the Turks. Now some members of the Holy League began to think of making peace with the Turks in order to defend themselves against the predatory French. By more Herculean efforts of diplomacy and persuasion, Pope Innocent managed to arrange an armistice that caused Louis to subside — at least temporarily.

With Catholic forces now more or less united, the Ottomans were forced to fight a great campaign on three fronts simultaneously: the Adriatic, Polish Ukraine, and Hungary. While all this was going on, Mehmed IV was fooling around with hunting and ignoring demands that he pay attention to the ongoing disintegration of his empire. Christian armies rolled through Hungary, sweeping the Turks from the lands they had held for nearly two centuries. Mass was once more celebrated in the great cathedral of Esztergom, which had long been a mosque. The ancient capital of Hungary, Buda, which had been called "the shield of Islam" by the Turks, was liberated in 1686, after a fierce and bloody seventy-eight day battle that involved defeating not only the occupiers of the city but a large Turkish relief force. The victory was complete, and the pasha of Buda died fighting bravely.

Father Marco d'Aviano called the liberation of Buda a real miracle. Volunteers had come from all over Europe, including France and England, to help the cause. A new grand vizier (Mehmed was going through them pretty fast) was defeated near Mohács, the site of the original Turkish victory over the royal Hungarian troops in 1526. The Ottoman army revolted after this new defeat and called for the grand vizier's execution. Mehmed complied, but by now exasperation with his incompetence had reached such a pitch that it was clearly his turn to go. He was declared deposed in November 1687 by the military and religious officials and lived as a prisoner for another five years. His half-brother, Suleiman II, was to last only four years, but he was at least an improvement.

The Last Rally of the Turks

Thanks to the upheaval in Turkish affairs, the liberation of Hungary continued. Legendary Eger was liberated in December 1687, and virtually the entire country of Hungary was free of the Turks by 1689. The Venetians liberated Athens in 1687, and

Belgrade, the key fort held by the Turks on the lower Danube, was freed in 1688. In that year, however, Emperor Leopold was forced to divert part of his army to deal with renewed aggression in the west from Louis XIV, while Louis' ambassador to the sultan urged his new grand vizier to make war on Leopold.

Köprülü III, as this latest grand vizier was called, was happy to oblige, and in 1690 he created a diversion in Transylvania while he himself advanced through Serbia to Belgrade, which he was able to surprise into surrender. It was late in the year so he did not follow up his success but returned to the capital. The next year he was back with an even larger army and met the army of Prince Louis. The grand vizier's officers advised delaying until Tartar reinforcements arrived, but the inexperienced Köprülü decided on attack. Bad decision. As the battle was going disastrously against the Turks, he made a last charge with his guards into the Austrian ranks, waving his sword and calling on Allah. He was shot dead, and his demoralized guards fled.

Thököly, the Ottoman puppet king, was still at large, however. He had supported the Turks at Vienna and shared in their debacle. He had then tried to make peace with Emperor Leopold, on terms that included being made prince of a large chunk of Hungary, which the emperor refused. So Thököly renewed his war against the Austrians and requested more Turkish help. Instead, his erstwhile Ottoman allies put him in chains and then into prison, probably for having negotiated with Leopold. He was let out to lead expeditions against Transylvania in 1686 and 1688 but both failed, so it was back to prison with him. In 1690 the Turks sent him out again with a larger army and he succeeded to the point of becoming prince of Transylvania. He could not maintain his rule there, however, and left the place the following year.

Zenta Turns the Tide

At the crucial battle of Zenta, on the river Tisza in Serbia, in 1697, the young general Eugene of Savoy and his army met a major Turkish offensive into Transylvania. The date was September 11. Eugene had marched his men all day and then threw them into battle — something the Turks had by no means expected. Furthermore, they were crossing the river at the time and were taken at a severe disadvantage. In the end the Turks lost about thirty thousand, killed in battle or drowned in the Tisza River, and several of the sultan's wives were captured. Eugene lost only 300 men. With the back of the Turkish army broken, the Ottomans were forced to sign the Treaty of Carlowitz in 1699 with their adversaries, Russia, Poland, Austria, and Venice.

By the terms of this treaty, Turkish attacks on Europe were brought to an end. Many of the Hungarians who fought with the Turks were offered amnesty, but it comes as no surprise to find Thököly[7] excluded by name. There were still areas remaining under Turkish control, including Belgrade (until 1717), some of which would not be liberated until World War I. Nonetheless the seventeenth-century crusade had freed most of occupied Central Europe, and saved the West from the threat that had hung over it for three hundred years. It was a spectacular success.

---

[7] This traitor and apostate would never get his due reward, on earth anyway. He would end up, after one more failed attack on Transylvania, living with his wife in Constantinople, much honored and rewarded by the sultan, until his death in 1705.

The Rest of the Story

We must bid farewell to the Ottoman Empire and its antagonists at Carlowitz, although volumes could be written (and have been) about the subsequent history of the empire, its subject peoples, and the ongoing consequences of its demise. The Christian resistance to the Ottoman conquest of Europe has been our theme, and at Carlowitz it triumphed.

That treaty represents a stage in the long decline of the Ottoman Empire that would end only with the establishment of modern Turkey in the twentieth century. Ottoman collapse was not, of course, a speedy implosion but a sort of zigzag roll downhill with a number of pauses. Throughout the eighteenth and nineteenth centuries the fading of the empire would be punctuated by some successes, as the state was modernized and some lost ground recovered — the conquest of Greek islands occupied by Venice, for example. Austria and Russia would get the better of the empire in the north, however, and the growth of nationalism in the Balkan states would lead to a series of wars and settlements in the nineteenth century that relentlessly reduced the empire's extent. Most European powers became concerned with the "Eastern Question" and how they might profit from the demise of what was soon being called "the sick man of Europe." Domestic political upheavals added to the stress on the remaining fragments of the Empire, and then, like our tale, it was finished.

Main Works Consulted

The New Cambridge Modern History, vols. V and VI. (New York: Cambridge University Press, 1961, 1970.)

Bradford, Ernle. *The Shield and the Sword.*

Carroll, Warren H. *A History of Christendom*, vol. IV.

Kinross, Lord. *The Ottoman Empire.* Quotation from Sokollu, p. 258.

Pastor, Ludwig von. *History of the Popes*, vols. XVIII and XXXII.

Seward, Desmond. *The Monks of War.*

Walsh, William Thomas. *Philip II.*

Ten

Islam at the Gates Once More

Now that the curtain has come down on Act Four, what conclusions can be drawn from the great drama of the jihad of the Ottoman Turks and its ultimate defeat?

As I tell my students, we base our judgments of historical events on their consequences, which fall into two broad categories: one includes the direct results and characteristics of something that has happened in history, such as who won a war and what effects the war had on the parties involved. The second — more important — category of historical judgments involves what I call the "so what?" questions: what is the significance of the event we have analyzed? What difference did it make to the world, and how relevant is it to us today? It remains to ask these questions about the Ottoman invasion of the West and its defeat.

Material Results of the Ottoman Conquests

In considering, first, the tangible results of the Ottoman conquests, we find that one of the obvious features of the period we have been examining is the extreme brutality of Turkish behavior, century after century. There was never any question of "just war" in their career; they simply moved into whatever areas they chose to conquer for Islam and Islamized them as far as they could. The conquests involved the cold-blooded murder of civilians: men, women, and children, the elderly and the sick. Hundreds of thousands, at the very least, were also enslaved, and sometimes used for human sacrifice. The Ottoman Empire was probably the greatest and most long-lasting slave empire in history, enslaving millions from Africa through the Near East. Millions of children were snatched from their families to serve purposes that ranged from the utilitarian to the depraved, and the fate of most of the women who became the property of soldiers or were imprisoned within harems is horrible to contemplate.

There seems to have been no respect for innocent human life, and in this the Muslim Turks differed radically from Christians. No one denies that Christians are as capable of atrocities as Muslims, but historically they have been restrained by the requirements of just warfare and by the Fifth Commandment, "Thou shalt not kill." As St. Thomas Aquinas taught Christians, "It is never lawful to kill the innocent," but at the hands of the Turks the innocent died in uncounted numbers. Those non-Muslims who did not die and would not convert (and there are examples of conversions being forced throughout most of Ottoman history) were subject to the discriminatory and humiliating requirements of *dhimmitude*, including heavy taxation, loss of their children, and destruction of their places of worship. The history of the Ottoman jihad also includes the martyrdom of large numbers of Christian priests, monks, and laity.[8]

---

[8] It is disconcerting to find that the same historians who often express horror at Tamerlane's pyramids of skulls, the Holocaust, and the Gulag, show little disapproval of equally horrible Ottoman practices.

The Role of Religion for Each Side in the Conflict

Another question raised by the events of the jihad and the anti-jihad is that of motivation: both for the original aggression of the Turks and for the resistance of so many generations of the conquered. The Ottomans' motivation certainly included thirst for power, love of warfare, and desire for loot. However none of these latter impulses, of themselves, would seem to account for the relentless and tenacious campaigns, century after century, against non-Muslim (and non-Sunni) countries, unless we add to them the desire to submit the world to Allah. The harsh and discriminatory treatment of the *dhimmi* throughout Ottoman history certainly had a religious origin, and reflects a particular set of religious principles.

As far as Western resistance goes, patriotism is sometimes cited as the main motive, and it was no doubt always present in the sentiment that the conquerors were "other," alien folk who did not belong in the land. (The modern cult of the nation, in the extreme form implied by the word "nationalism," is quite a recent phenomenon that does not apply to most of the period we have been examining.) Politics is also sometimes adduced as a force for resistance, since there were obvious cases of the desire for territorial independence or the need for border protection fueling combats against the Turks. Politics, however, cuts both ways; to many it seemed more politic to make peace with the occupier, even to embrace his religion, and thus have a certain share in his political system. Politics certainly influenced French and English rulers, and states such as Venice, to cooperate with and flatter the Ottomans, rather than to oppose them.

Venice and other mercantile regimes also cooperated for economic reasons. Their preoccupation with business above all, to the detriment of the defense of Christendom, is distressing to find in a Christian state. It also seems amazingly shortsighted: "When the time comes to hang capitalists," said Lenin, "they will be selling us the rope." He might have been speaking of the Venetians before they woke up to find themselves Ottoman targets, fighting a desperate war for Candia. There is considerable ambiguity in the Venetian attitude, however, and often in the whole European context of how the Turks should be dealt with.

One is left with religion as the essential mainspring of the resistance; everywhere, those who led the liberation struggles and those who followed them identified themselves as Christian. Some were fervently so and some nominally so, but the overwhelming majority of the kings, generals, preachers, victims of the Turks, and ordinary foot soldiers of the resistance in Europe and North Africa were Christian, either Orthodox or Catholic, as were those who died as martyrs for the Faith. (The ambiguity of the Protestant position has been noted in earlier chapters.)

Religion alone, however, would not have been enough had it not been allied with politics. In a 1951 article entitled "How Europe was Saved," Abbé Georges de Nantes analyzed the fifth-century resistance of Gaul to the barbarian invasions, in particular that of the Huns. He observed that the victory was won through a combination of the staunch faith of the population allied with military force and diplomacy (as when Pope St. Leo the Great negotiated the withdrawal of the Huns from Italy). Faith could not by itself defeat the barbarians except insofar as it acted through both politics and military strength, and they in turn needed the spiritual impetus of militant Christianity.

This points up the tragedy of Christendom throughout the Ottoman period. Faith had grown too tepid to motivate the rulers of Europe to the sacrifice of their local political and economic interests. Even the popes of the period we have surveyed, with a few shining exceptions, behaved in practical matters more like Italian princes, and opulent ones at that, than vicars of Christ. Their local political roles often prevented them from being able to rally the states with which they were so often at odds politically. Even St. Pius V was able to get support for the fleet that sailed to Lepanto from only a handful of states.

The common people were another story. In them, the Faith was still alive. That they could still be moved to sacrifice the little they had by going on crusade is proved by the success of St. John Capistrano's preaching of the Crusade of Belgrade, as well as by the response to the preachers sent out by Pope Pius II to preach the Crusade of Mantua. Ordinary men flocked to Belgrade and to Ancona, but they needed a Hunyadi — or at least some military chief — to lead them. It was the leaders that so often let them down, due both to lack of faith and indifference to the plight of fellow Christian nations. Even the self-interest of these leaders was shortsighted, since it was focused on short-term gains in political power rather than security from invasion.

Only the rulers of Spain, drawing on their own experience of Islamic occupation, seem to have consistently mustered the will to join the anti-jihad to the extent that they could. It is galling to reflect that the Balkans and Hungary need not have suffered under Turkish control for so many centuries, and the Faith would not have been lost in so many souls, had Europe remained fervently Christian. The Age of Faith was already dying, however, by the time the Ottoman invasion began in earnest. Indeed, the very idea of Christendom itself — a spiritual body transcending its individual nation-members — was gone by the early modern period, seemingly forever. When, at the very last minute, Europe rallied enough energy to roll up the Ottoman Empire like a Turkish carpet, the spirit was only partially that of crusade, and that mostly in the early days. Although religious freedom was also one of their goals in fighting for liberation, by the eighteenth century modern nationalism too was beginning to develop within the submerged peoples of the Ottoman Empire. The major Western powers had designs on what rapidly became known as "the sick man of Europe," and early in the twentieth century they carved up most of the empire among themselves — thereby causing more problems than they solved, like the antagonisms unleashed in the Balkans among the newly liberated.

The Communist Parallel

One may well wonder whether today's de-Christianized West would be able to summon up the energy to resist anything like the Ottoman conquest. A possible historical parallel to Europe's response to the Turks, though an imperfect one, may be found in the West's reaction to the spread of atheistic Communism. When it first emerged in Russia in 1917, Prime Minister Churchill urged military action by the Western powers to crush what he saw as a great peril for the world. The small expeditionary force that was actually sent, however, did not receive whole-hearted support from the participating nations, including the United States. It was soon withdrawn, having achieved nothing more than reinforcement of Lenin's belief in Western flabbiness. The starvation of the Ukraine produced no Western reaction, nor did the gradual Communist takeover of Central and Eastern Europe and much of the Balkans. Countries such as Hungary, which had suffered nearly two hundred years of Turkish occupation, now fell under an even worse regime for half a century, with no Western intervention even during the gallant and doomed Hungarian Revolution of 1956.

In the case of Communism, as with the Turkish conquests, the elimination of Christianity was a major element of the agenda of the conquerors, and its defense equally important to most of the conquered. Like the anti-Ottoman movement, anti-Communism was largely religious and produced many martyrs, though patriotism and economic factors were not absent from its program. There is this difference between the rise and fall of the Ottoman and Communist empires: in the case of the Turks, the papacy continually preached the crusade, albeit mostly to deaf ears, and a few glorious examples of crusading enterprises actually occurred. There was none of that in the case of opposition to the Communist empire. (Even the papacy's later criticisms were muted, for whatever reasons.)

In the modern West, faced with a Communist empire reaching into Germany and the Baltic coast, there was not even a whisper of crusade. In a nuclear age the stakes were too high, the economy would suffer, other political issues loomed larger, and more-secularized Europe and America seemed willing to sacrifice half of Christendom in the exchange. It was not only faith that was wanting, of course, but charity also; the supernatural charity that would take pity on the souls, like the Christian slaves languishing on the Barbary Coast centuries earlier, waiting for liberation from a cruel and atheistic regime. Lacking those virtues, despite its wealth and power the West did even less against the Communist regimes that enslaved Christendom for decade after decade than it had done against the Ottomans.

The "So What" Question: Relevance for Today

Could there ever be a real revival of the kind of Islamic menace represented historically by the Ottoman Empire? The possibility seems farfetched. After all, the World War I peace settlements carved up the Middle East, formerly ruled by the Ottomans, into European "mandates" and miscellaneous states with questionable borders, and these have remained more or less in place. Most Europeans, who had for centuries identified the Muslim threat to the West with Ottoman power, considered that that menace at least was finished for good, and that seems to have been the mainstream view until quite recently.

Hilaire Belloc, however, was already disagreeing with it in 1936, the year in which he wrote an essay entitled "The Great and Enduring Heresy of Mohammed," which he included two years later in his book, *The Great Heresies*. After surveying the undeniable collapse of Muslim political power following World War I, he wrote:

> It would seem . . . as though the great duel was now decided. But can we be certain it is so decided? I doubt it very much. It has always seemed to me possible, and even probable, that there would be a resurrection of Islam and that our sons or our grandsons would see the renewal of that tremendous struggle between the Christian culture and what has been for more than a thousand years its greatest opponent . . . I cannot but believe that a main unexpected thing of the future is the return of Islam.

He goes on to examine the reasons often given in support of the contrary conviction. He cites, for example, the opinion that the Muslim doctrine of fatalism induces political inertia, but dismisses it on the obvious grounds that "fatalism" certainly did not get in the way of the great Muslim empire-building of the previous ages. Nineteenth-century observers also detected a fatal flaw in the tendency to disruption and disunity that seemed to plague Muslim states. Belloc acknowledges this "fissiparous" characteristic, but notes that the fragments have also demonstrated a capacity to unite suddenly and effectively under a strong leader, and he speculates that Islamic resurgence will recur in just such a manner:

> There is no leader as yet, but enthusiasm might bring one and there are signs enough in the political heavens today of what we may have to expect from the revolt of Islam at some future date — perhaps not far distant.

Belloc also acknowledges that early twentieth-century Muslim countries were technologically backward by comparison with the West, and had been so for a long time. He remarks astutely, however, that such backwardness was not inherent to Islam, since in the heyday of Ottoman power Turkish armaments, ships, and technology were often superior to those of the West. He concludes, "there is no reason whatever why [Islamic culture] should not learn its new lesson and become our equal in all those temporal things which now *alone* give us our superiority over it. . . ."

Why does he emphasize "alone"? It is to emphasize our peril if technological superiority is all we have to depend upon. For him, the key point is that the West has lost its *religious* energy, without which no great culture has ever arisen or long survived. The nationalism that acted for a time as a substitute for religion in the later stages of the wars of liberation against the Turks soon declined, like the Christianity it attempted to replace:

> In Islam, there has been no such dissolution of ancestral doctrine — or at least nothing corresponding to the universal break-up of religion in Europe. The whole spiritual strength of Islam is still present in the masses of Syria and Anatolia, of the East Asian

mountains, of Arabia, Egypt and North Africa. The final fruit of
this tenacity, the second period of Islamic power, may be delayed
— but I doubt whether it can be permanently postponed.

This analysis hardly seems dated by seventy years; it might
have been written yesterday, and its conclusion is supported by
a number of contemporary observers. True, Bernard Lewis has
observed that since the defeat of the Ottoman jihad at Vienna
in 1683, no Muslim country has posed the kind of threat to
Christendom that the Turks did. On the other hand, Bat Ye'or,
in *Eurabia*, sees the Muslim world becoming "ever more united
under an Islamist, anti-Western ideology," whereas "Europe has
been neutralized from within by EAD [Euro-Arab Dialogue]
policy and by internal Islamist terror, which has also silenced
and intimidated Muslim reformists." Her book is both polemical
and highly controversial, as she traces the political, economic,
and cultural developments of the last decades that have con-
ditioned Europeans to what she calls "passive *dhimmi* surrender." Particularly unsettling is a chapter on "The Islamization of
Christianity," dealing — among other topics — with misleading
interpretations of Islam introduced into Muslim-Christian dialogue, the plight of Palestinian Christianity, the real Muslim view
of Christianity and Christian history and how it is portrayed in
Muslim textbooks.

On the Muslim side Moammar Gadhafi, in a speech broadcast
in the spring of 2006, boasted that "the fifty million Muslims
of Europe will turn it into a Muslim continent within a few
decades" — and do it "without swords, without guns, without
conquests." The Muslim presence in Europe was accomplished
"without conquests" because the galloping depopulation of the
West — a product of de-Christianization and a hedonist lifestyle
that excludes children — has made the importation of a foreign

labor force necessary. High Muslim birthrates in many Western countries have given rise to a new and ambitious generation of young Muslims, some of whom have proclaimed their intention of attaining political power to achieve Islamic goals in their adopted countries. (This recalls the original spread of Islam outside the Arabian Peninsula through immigration; it also echoes the takeover of the old Roman Empire by overwhelming barbarian immigration.) The tough and militant leaders of Kosovo are not likely to be content until one more independent Muslim state has been inserted into Europe, and there have even been recent proposals to establish *sharia* law in Canada.

A Dutch editor recently wrote,

> When I was growing up, we made a laughingstock of the Roman Catholic Church — but when the Islamicists began to come, we stopped making those religious jokes. Nobody said anything against Islam. We were all cowards.

Anxious over economic and demographic realities, and having traded the Faith for multiculturalism, the West indeed seems cowed by the growing Islamic presence within it, and almost pathetically anxious to placate Muslim sensibilities. British and Dutch schools remove books about pigs from school libraries (and banks no longer distribute piggy banks to their customers) and purge mention of the Holocaust from history classes. Muslim soldiers in the Austrian army refuse to salute their flag, and are not disciplined for it. Many Western countries are mandating special public accommodations for Muslims — for example, prayer rooms and ritual footbaths for Muslim college students — even while their courts ban nativity sets and Christmas carols from schools. Meanwhile, the Muslim population in the West is not only burgeoning, but increasingly militant. A Dutch politician who decried Muslim immigration is murdered; gangs of

Muslim youths from Australia to Scandinavia are implicated in an epidemic of horrible rapes; rocks fly and cars burn in the Muslim ghettoes that now envelop the heart of Paris.

From Belloc to Gadhafi, and from contemporary researchers like Bat Ye'or, the West has been periodically warned for the last seventy years that a new Islamic offensive is looming, and there are signs that it has already begun. Whether it will be a violent one, as Belloc thought, or peaceful, as in Gadhafi's view, remains to be seen. Either way, it must be of vital concern to us whether we in fact come under Muslim domination; it certainly wasn't pleasant the last time. It looks as if Act Five has begun, and it is by no means clear if it will have a happy ending. Perhaps, in the end, it will be only by a miracle of grace and the conversion of Islam, which the saints and popes like Pius II never ceased to hope for, that the threat can be neutralized. Dialogue and groveling won't do it, and we seem to have little else to offer.

Main Works Consulted

Belloc, Hilaire. *The Great Heresies.*

Lewis, Bernard. *The Middle East.*

Ye'or, Bat. *Eurabia.*

Select Bibliography

Note: The following is a list of the major works used in writing this book, whether for general background or specific details. In the *Works Consulted* sections that follow each chapter, sources are referenced only by author and book title.

Islamic Religion and Culture

Bonnet-Eymard, Brother Bruno. *Le Coran: Traduction et Commentaire Systématique.* (Saint-Parres-lès-Vaudes: Maison Saint-Joseph, 1988, 1990, 1997, for the three volumes that have so far appeared. The explanatory essays accompanying the translation proper have been very useful. I have also utilized the articles on Islam by Brother Bruno in the periodical *Il Est Réssuscité*; its English Web site is http://www.crc-internet.org/

Belloc, Hilaire. *The Great Heresies.* (Manassas, Virginia: Trinity Communications, 1987 — first published 1938.) Interesting observations on Islam.

Bolton, Andrew G., M.D., editor. *The Legacy of Jihad: Islamic Holy War and the Fate of Non-Muslims.* (Amherst, New York: Prometheus Books, 2005.) A large collection of articles and primary documents dealing with the book's topics. I found the primary source material particularly valuable.

Lewis, Bernard. *The Arabs in History*. (New York: Harper &
   Row, 1967.)

———. *The Middle East*. (New York: Simon & Schuster, 1997.)

———. *What Went Wrong?* (New York: Oxford University
   Press, 2002.)

Davis, Robert C. *Christian Slaves and Muslim Masters*. (New
   York: Palgrave Macmillan, 2003.)

Warraq, Ibn, editor. *What the Koran Really Says*. (Amherst, New
   York: Prometheus Books, 2002.) Another useful compilation
   of scholarly articles and translations.

Ye'or, Bat. *The Decline of Eastern Christianity Under Islam:
   From Jihad to Dhimmitude*. (Cranbury, New Jersey: Associated University Presses, 1996; original French edition
   1991.)

———. *Eurabia*. (Cranbury, New Jersey: Associated University
   Presses, 2006.)

———. *Juifs et Chrétiens sous l'Islam*. (Paris: Berg International,
   1994.)

The Ottoman Empire

Many articles in various volumes of the *The Cambridge Mod-
ern History*, especially Chapter III, "The Ottoman Empire," by
J. B. Bury in vol. I, *The Renaissance* (New York: The Macmillan
Company, 1907). Articles in *The New Cambridge Modern His-
tory*, vols. V and VI. (New York: Cambridge University Press,
1961, 1970.) Numerous sections of vols. V, VI, and VII of
The New Cambridge Medieval History. (New York: Cambridge
University Press, 1998.)

Aubenas, Roger, and Ricard, Robert. *L'Eglise et la Renaissance* (vol. XV of the Fliche et Martin *Histoire de l'Eglise.*) (Paris: Bloud & Gay, 1951.)

Darras, J. E. and Bareille, J. *Histoire de l'Eglise*, vols. XXXI and XXXII. (Paris: Louis Vivès, 1884.)

Dawson, Christopher, editor. *The Mongol Mission*. (New York: Sheed and Ward, 1955.) A collection of primary texts and an excellent introduction; useful for the role played by the Mongols in Ottoman history.

Goodwin, Jason. *Lords of the Horizons*. (New York: Henry Holt and Company, 1999.) This could be a useful introduction to Ottoman history, provided the reader is prepared to double-check all the information in it. Much of it is erroneous and the sources of direct quotations are often not cited. I have used it for a broad overview and one or two anecdotes.

Hegyi, Klára and Zimányi, Vera. *The Ottoman Empire in Europe*. (Budapest: Corvina, 1989.) Some interesting information about local conditions for people conquered by the Turks, but without citing any specific references. The main value of the work is the great number of photographs of maps, buildings, and art objects.

Kinross, Lord. *The Ottoman Empire*. (London: The Folio Society, 2003 [first published 1977].)

Rossi, Father Rossi, *et al. The Custody of the Holy Land*. (Jerusalem: Custody of the Holy Land Editions, 1981.) An overview and history of Holy Land sites and the work of the Custody.

The Byzantine Empire

Baynes, N. H., and Moss, H. St. L. B., editors. *Byzantium: An Introduction to East Roman Civilization.* (Oxford: The Clarendon Press, 1961 [first published 1948].) A good collection of articles by scholars on various aspects of Byzantine history.

Diehl, Charles. *Byzantium: Greatness and Decline,* English translation. (New Brunswick, New Jersey: Rutgers University Press, 1957.)

Vasiliev, A. A. *History of the Byzantine Empire,* vol. II. (Madison and Milwaukee: University of Wisconsin Press, 1964.) An excellent and well-documented survey of Byzantine history.

Vryonis, Speros, Jr. *The Decline of Medieval Hellenism in Asia Minor and the Process of Islamization from the Eleventh through the Fifteenth Century.* (Berkeley, Los Angeles, London: University of California Press, 1986.)

Hungary and the Balkans

The Balkans

Fine, John V. A., Jr. *The Late Medieval Balkans.* (Ann Arbor: The University of Michigan Press, 1987.) This is an indispensable work for understanding the unbelievably complex affairs of the Balkan Peninsula from the end of the twelfth century through the Ottoman conquest. The marvel is that it is so readable.

Hungary

Gárdonyi, Géza. *The Eclipse of the Crescent Moon.* Translation of *Egri Csillagok*. (Budapest: Corvina Books, 1997.) This is a wonderful historical novel of which the climax is the siege of Eger. I have included it only because the author did extensive research in the Hungarian, Turkish, Latin, and German sources, consulting documents in Vienna and Constantinople as well as Hungary, and his description of the siege seems generally accurate. The English translation reads well except for some incoherencies of liturgical terminology.

Halecki, Oscar. *Borderlands of Western Civilization: A History of East Central Europe.* (New York: The Ronald Press Company, 1952.) An older work by a fine Polish Catholic scholar.

Held, Joseph. *Hunyadi: Legend and Reality.* (New York: Eastern European Monographs and Columbia University Press, 1985.) A short biography of the great Hungarian hero and the people of his time.

Johnson, Lonnie R. *Central Europe.* (New York, Oxford: Oxford University Press, 1996.)

Komjathy, Anthony Tihamer. *A Thousand Years of the Hungarian Art of War.* (Toronto: Rakoczi Foundation, 1982.)

Macartney, C. A. M. *Hungary.* (Edinburgh: The Edinburgh University Press, 1962.) Macartney was perhaps the most accomplished British specialist in Hungarian history of his generation and his book is still worth reading as an introduction.

Peres, Géza. *The Fall of the Medieval Kingdom of Hungary: Mohács 1526–Buda 1541.* (Boulder, Colorado: Social Science Monographs, 1989.)

Sinor, Denis. *History of Hungary.* (New York: Frederick A. Praeger, 1959.)

Sugar, Peter F., *et al. A History of Hungary.* (Bloomington and Indianapolis: Indiana University Press, 1990.) Another survey by a number of historians.

Vardy, S. B., *et al.*, editors. *Louis the Great, King of Hungary and Poland.* (New York: Eastern European Monographs and Columbia University Press, 1986.) A collection of articles in several languages on the reign of this important monarch.

Zombori, István, *et al. A Thousand Years of Christianity in Hungary.* (Budapest: The Hungarian Catholic Episcopal Conference, 2001.) Very useful collection of articles on many aspects of Hungarian Catholic history by scholars in the field.

Greece and the Mediterranean Islands

Bradford, Ernle. *The Shield and the Sword: The Knights of St. John, Jerusalem, Rhodes, and Malta.* (New York: E. P. Dutton & Co., Inc., 1973.)

Ettelsdorf, Raymond. *The Soul of Greece.* (Westminster, Maryland: The Newman Press, 1963.)

Pavlidis, Vangelis. *Rhodes 1306–1522: A Story.* (Rhodes: Rodos Image, 1999 ? [undated except for introduction.]) This is an odd book to appear in a scholarly bibliography, and yet it is full of solid detailed history on the Island of the Knights. The author, a native of Rhodes, was a political cartoonist when he became seriously interested in researching the island's history and writing an account copiously illustrated with detailed renderings of weapons, battlements, topographical sketches, and even humorous cartoons. The work is recommended by a leading Byzantine scholar and I have found in it considerable information — from the Rhodian point of view — about the Knights, the Turkish sieges, and much else.

Seward, Desmond. *The Monks of War*. (London: The Folio Society, 2000.) A revised edition of a work originally published in 1972; it is a general history of the military orders, especially useful for the Mediterranean battles fought by the Hospitallers, including Rhodes and Malta.

The Church and the Papacy

Hughes, Philip, Msgr. *The Church in Crisis — the Twenty Great Councils*. (London: Burns & Oates, 1960.)

Pastor, Ludwig von. *History of the Popes*. (London: various publishers from 1891 on) 40 volumes. This tremendous work of scholarship combines narrative history with copious notes and many previously unpublished documents. It is indispensable, though not infallible, for any researcher dealing with papal affairs from the fourteenth through the eighteenth centuries, and I have consulted portions of the several volumes dealing with the topic of this book.

Pius II, Pope. *Memoirs of a Renaissance Pope: The Commentaries of Pius II*. (New York: Capricorn Books, 1962.) This is

an abridged version of the diaries of Aeneas Sylvius Piccolomini, before and after he became pope. I used it especially
for his account of the struggle with the Turkish and his own
strong desire to liberate the conquered Christian lands.

General Histories of Christendom

Carroll, Warren H. *A History of Christendom*, vols. III and IV.
(Front Royal: Christendom Press, 1993, 2000.)

Daniel-Rops, Henri. *History of the Church of Christ*, vol. II of
*The Church in the Seventeenth Century; The Church in the
Eighteenth Century*. (New York: Image Books, 1965, 1966.)

Rulers, Saints, Miscellaneous Historical Works

Braudel, Fernand. *The Perspective of the World*, vol. III. *Civilization and Capitalism, 15th–18th Century*. (New York: Harper
& Row, 1984.)

Carroll, Warren H. *Isabel of Spain: The Catholic Queen*. (Front
Royal: Christendom Press, 1991.)

Coste, Pierre, C.M. *The Life and Works of St. Vincent de Paul*,
(Three Volumes.) (Westminster, Maryland: The Newman
Press, 1952.)

Crankshaw, Edward. *Maria Theresa*. (New York: The Viking
Press, 1970.)

Hofer, John, Rev. *St. John Capistran, Reformer*. (St. Louis and
London: B. Herder Book Company, 1943.)

Janssen, Jean. *L'Allemagne et la Réforme*, vol. III. (Paris: E. Plon, Nourrit et Cie, 1892.)

Kann, Robert A. *A History of the Habsburg Empire, 1526–1918.* (Berkeley, Los Angeles, London: University of California Press, 1977.)

Walsh, William Thomas. *Philip II.* (New York: Sheed & Ward, Inc., 1937. Reprinted, TAN Books and Publishers, Inc. 1987.)

Index

Abraham, 6
Actium, Battle of, 193
Adrian VI, Pope, 166
Adrianople, 56, 63
Aeneas Sylvius Piccolomini, 55,
    76, 88, see also Pius II
Ahmad, son of Bayazid II, 129
Albania, 56–58, 61–62, 77, 83,
    86–89, 104, 107–12
Albertus Magnus, St., 13
Alexander VI, Pope, 126
Alexander VII, Pope, 182
Ali, Uluj, 194
almsgiving, 5
Amadeus VI, Count of Savoy,
    32, 36
Anatolia, 29, 32, 43–46, 52, 63
Angelovich, Michael, 94
Apafi, Prince, 203
Aquinas, St. Thomas, 13, 216
Archangelos, Maria, 116
Arab conquests, 10–12
Arpàd, Hungarian House of,
    161
Austrians, 161–62, 172–75,
    179, 188, 191, 194, 201–5,
    210–12, 225

Bakócz, Cardinal, 163
banats, 31
Balkans, 83ff.

Baphaeon, Battle of, 24
Barbarossa, Kheir-ed-din, 141–
    43, 146–50, 153
Barbary Coast, 142–44, 146–
    47, see also slavery
Bashi-Bazouks, 116, 119, 140
Basle, Council of, 96
Bayazid I, Sultan, (the Thunder-
    bolt), 44–52, 54
Bayazid II, Sultan, 123–29,
    185–86
Bedouins, 14, 19
Belgrade, 75–81
Belloc, Hilaire, 222–23
Berbers, 12, 19–20
Bey, Orhan, see Orhan I
Bey, Osman, see Osman I
Bey, Suleyman, see Suleyman,
    Pasha
Black Death, 36
Blackbirds, Field of, 45–46
Bogomil, 95
Boleyn, Anne, 133
Bonnet-Eymard, Br. Bruno, 6, 22
Borgia, St. Francis, 191, see also
    Society of Jesus
Bornemissza, Gergely, 176
Bosnia, 43, 45–46, 83, 89, 91,
    95–100, 103, 112–13, 160
Boucicaut, Marshal of France,
    49–50, 52, 66

boy tribute, see devşirme
Bragadino, General, 190,
    192
Brankovic, George, (Djuradj),
    King of Serbia, 56, 59–60,
    92–93, 97
Brankovic, Lazar, King of Serbia,
    92–95
Buda, 164–68, 170–71, 173,
    175, 178–79, 201, 209
Bull of the Crusade, 90
Burgundy, John of, 47
Burgio, Baron, 166–68
Byzantines, 27, 30, 33, 64, 69
Byzantium, religious disarray in,
    8–9, 63

Callistus III, Pope, 76
Calvinists, 201, 203
Campeggio, Cardinal-Legate,
    167
Candia, War of, 197–99, 204,
    218
Cantacuzene, John VI, Byzantine
    Emperor, 27
Capistrano, St. John, 78–80,
    219
Carletti de Chivasso, Bl. Angelo,
    121, 122
Carlowitz, Treaty of, (1699),
    211–12
Castriot, George, see Skanderbeg
Castriot, John, ruler of Epirus,
    56
Cesarini, Cardinal, 60
Chania, 151
Charles, Duke of Lorraine,
    (Prince), 203, 205–6

Charles IV, Holy Roman Em-
    peror, 36
Charles V, Holy Roman Em-
    peror, 133, 141, 148–50, 154,
    164–66, 171, 173, 187
Charles VI, King of France, 49
Charles VIII, King of France,
    126
Charles IX, King of France, 191
Chivasso, Blessed Angelo
    Carletti de, 121–22, 156–
    57
Clairvaux, St. Bernard of, 33
Claver, St. Peter, 148
Clement VII, Pope, 166–67
Clement IX, Pope, 199
Clement X, Pope, 182
Communism, 39, 71, 74, 220–
    21
Conciliarism, 54
Constantine I of Rome, (the
    Great), 75
Constantine IV,
Constantine IX, 85
Constantine XI, 64, 66, 70
Constantinople, 9, 23–24, 30,
    32, 34–37, 47, 50, 53, 55,
    63–75, 83–86, 91–92
Corfu, 192
Corvinus, Matyas, King of
    Hungary, 89, 94, 99, 103,
    125, 170
Council of Florence, see Union
    of Florence
Croatia, 83, 99, 103–4, 128,
    201
Cromwell, Oliver, 65, 197
Crusades, 19–21, 23–24, 33,

47, 49, 55, 57, 68, 88–92, 95, 105, 161, 219

D'Amaral, Grand Chancellor Andrea, 138–40
D'Aubusson, Grand Master Pierre, 115, 116–18, 124
D'Aviano, Marco, Fr., 206, 209
Dalmatia, 99, 128, 198
Damascene, St. John, 8
dar-al-harb, 15
Dardanelles, 27–28, 32, 49
De Medici, Marie, 191
De Rocas, Amalda, 189
De la Valette, Jean Parisot, Grand Master, 154–57
Delos, 152
Demetrius, son of John VIII, Byzantine Emperor, 85–88
Demotika, Battle of, 27
Devşirme, 37–39, 45, 53, 101, 140, 160
dhimmi, dhimmitude, 15–18, 26, 84, 160, 216–17
Diet of Poland, 202
Diet of Speyer, 166, 171
Diet of Worms, 165
Diez, Blas, 138–39
Djandarh, Hahl, 84
Djem, son of Mehemmed II, 123–27
Dobó, Istvan, 176–77
Domitian, Roman Emperor, 151
Don Juan of Austria, 188, 191–93, 195–96
Doria, Admiral Giovanni Andrea, 142, 149, 192

Dracula, *see* Vlad the Impaler
Dragut, 153–54, 156
Ducas, historian, 72, 82
Dušan, Stephen, Serb leader, 92

EAD [Euro-Arab Dialogue], 224
Eger, Siege of, 175–78, 209
Elias, Monastery of, 152
Elizabeth of Hungary, St., 161
Elizabeth, Queen of England, 191, 196
Elmo, St., fort of Rhodes, 155–56
Esztergom, 173, 209
Eugenius IV, Pope, 55

Famagusta, 189, 192
Ferdinand, Archduke, 170
Ferrante of Naples, 125
filioque controversy, 55
Francis I, King of France, 131, 133, 150, 165, 191
Frederick III, Holy Roman Emperor, 76

Gadhafi, Moammar, 224, 226
galleasses, 193–95
Gallipoli, 28, 36–37
gaza, ghazi, 25, 29, 75, *see also Jihad*
Genoa, 66, 68, 107, 191, 208
Granada, 17, 187–88
Great Schism, 44, 53–54
Greece, 84–88
Gregory VII, Pope St., 20, 90
Guadalupe, Our Lady of, 192

Habsburgs, 103–4, 133, 142,
    161, 165, 170–71, 173, 180–
    82, 199, 201, 208
Hagar, 6
Hagia Sophia, 64, 66, 69–71, 73
harems, 3, 17, 63, 71, 88, 142,
    149, 153, 197, 200, 203,
    216
Helen, (Palaeologova), Queen of
    Serbia, 94–95
Hellespont, *see* Dardanelles
Henry IV, King of England, 145
Henry VI, King of England, 76
Henry VIII, King of England,
    131, 133, 154
Herceg, ("Duke"), *see* Vukcic,
    Stefan
Hercegovina, 99, 111
Holy League, 191–92, 194, 196,
    202, 208
Hospitaller, Knights of St. John,
    32, 47–48, 113–15, 137–40,
    153–54, 156
human sacrifice, 44–45, 216
Hundred Years' War, 36, 47, 52
Huns, 218
Hunyadi, Janos, 56–58, 60, 78–
    79, 81, 94, 101–2, 219
Hunyadi, Matyas, *see* Corvinus,
    Matyas
Hussites, (John Hus), 54, 96

Ibrahim, Grand Vizier, 168, 185
Ibrahim, Pasha, 204
Ibrahim I, Sultan, 197–98
içoglan, 38
imam, 130, 132
Imre, St., 161

Innocent VIII, Pope, 125–26
Innocent XI, Pope Bl., 199, 202,
    208
Isabella, Queen of Spain, 120,
    143
Ishmael, 6
Isidore, Cardinal, 64, 70–71
Iskander beg, *see* Skanderbeg
Islam, emergence of, 4–6
    culture, 12–13
    relations with non-Muslims,
        see dhimmi, dhimmitude
Islamization, 29, 58, 224–25
Istanbul, *see* Constantinople

Janissaries, 38–39, 118, 124,
    129, 138, 140, 155, 169, 172,
    177, 180, 206
Januarius, St., 118
Jervis, Roger, 117
Jesuits, *see* Society of Jesus
Jihad, 7, 14–15, 21, 25, 29, 36,
    60, 71, 75, 84, 215–17, 219,
    224
Jizya, 14
John V, Byzantine Emperor,
    (Palaeologus), 30, 33, 36,
    115
John VIII, Byzantine Emperor,
    53–54, 85

Kaaba, 130
Knights of Malta, 194, 208, *see
    also* Hospitaller, Knights
Kolonitsch, Count (bishop of
    Wiener-Neustadt), 204
Koran, *see* Qur'an
Kosovo, Battles of, 45, 78

Köszeg, 173
Kroja, Siege of, 110–11
Kurtoglu, Admiral, 137–38
L'Isle, Philippe Villiers de, Grand
  Master, 136–37
Lajos the Great, King of Hun-
  gary, 31, 36
Lajos II, of Hungary, 163, 167,
  169–70
Laszlo, King of Hungary, 161
Lateran, Fifth Council of, 131
Lazar I, Ruler of Serbia, 45–46
Lazar II, (Brankovic), Ruler of
  Serbia, 92–95
Lenin, Vladimir Ilyich, 218, 220
Leo I, Pope St., (the Great), 218
Leo X, Pope, 130, 164
Leopold, Emperor, 201, 210
Lepanto, 128, 185, 193–96, 219
Lorraine, Duke of, 203, 205–6
Louis IX, King of France, 20
Louis XIII, King of France, 197
Louis XIV, King of France, (the
  Sun King), 182, 197, 200–1,
  208, 210
Luther, Martin, 131, 133, 164,
  166, 171

Magyars, 78, 160
Malta, 141–42, 152–57, 178,
  191, 198, 204, 208
Mamluks, 34
Manicheans, 95
Mantegna, Andrea, 127
Mantua, Crusade (Congress) of,
  89, 219
Manuel II, Byzantine Emperor,
  34–35, 41, 47, 49–50, 53

Maria the Dancer, 194
Martel, Charles, (the Hammer),
  12
Martinuzzi, George, 173
Maximilian I, Holy Roman
  Emperor, 131
Mehemmed II, Sultan, 53, 63–
  64, 67–70, 73, 75, 77, 79,
  83–88, 90, 92, 94, 101–4,
  107–15, 119–23, 130, 132–
  33
Mehmed IV, Sultan, 198, 200–1,
  208–9
Mekcsey, Deputy Commander,
  177
Meingre, Jean, *see* Boucicaut
Messina, 192
mihrabs, 71
Minorca, 150
Mohács, 165, 167, 169–71,
  180–81, 209
Moldavia, 100–3
Mongols, 15, 23, 51–53
Monophysites, 8, 26
Monothelites, 8
Montserrat, Our Lady of, 149
Morea, 67, 77, 85–86
muezzin, 140
Murad I, Sultan, 34, 37, 40, 45–
  46
Murad II, Sultan, 56–57, 59–60,
  83–84
Murad III, Sultan, 196
Muslim, see Islam
Mustafa I, Lala, Sultan, 185,
  188–90
Mustafa II, Kara, Sultan, 200–1,
  203–7

Nestorians, 8, 51
Nicopolis, Battle of, 47–48, 51
Notaras, Duke Lukas, 73– 74

Orhan I, (Bey), 24, 26–28, 31,
    37, 114
Osman I, (Bey), 23, 24–25, 114
Ottoman Empire, 23–32
Otranto, 120–22

Palaeologus, *see* John V, Em-
    peror of Constantinople
Pantaleon, St., feast of, 118–19
Parisot, Grand Master Jean, *see*
    De la Valette
Pasha of Buda, 178
Pasha, Ibrahim, 204
Pasha, Misac, 115, 117–19
Pasha, Piali, 188
Patmos, 151
Pail III, Pope, 149
Pavia, Battle of, 165
pederasty, 38
Pelbrát of Temesvár, 162
Peloponnese, *see* Morea
Petrarch, 32
Phillip II, King of Spain, 188,
    196
pontoon bridge, 117
Pius II, Pope, 55, 76, 87–91,
    98–99, 109, 113, 219, 226
Pius IV, Pope, 154
Pius V, Pope St., 157, 191–95
Protestant revolt of Hungary,
    201–3
Protestantism, 65, 131, 154,
    161, 166, 171, 174, 181,
    182, 191, 201

Qur'an, 5–8, 11, 14–15, 155,
    182, 186

Ramadan, 5
razzias, 11
Reformation, Protestant, 65,
    154, 161, 170, 197
Reconquista, Spanish (1492), 12
Rhodes, Sieges of, 113–19, 135–
    41
Richelieu, Cardinal, 197
Romania, *see* Wallachia
Rosary, 192
Rosary, Our Lady of the, 195
Roxelana, wife of Suleiman I,
    178, 185–86
Rumeli, 45–46, 63–64

sack of Constantinople, 24
sackers, sacking, 24, 118, 149–
    50, 189
Sandoval, Fr., 148
Santorini, 3, 152
schismatic Christians, 32, 34,
    64, 74
Scolarius, Gennadius, 71–72
Selim I, (the Grim), 129–33,
    136, 141–42, 185
Selim II the Sot (the Drunkard),
    186, 187–88, 190, 195–96
Seljuq Turks, 15, 19–21, 23–24,
    26, 51
sharia, 225
Serbia, 59–60, 93–95
Sheba, Queen of, 5
Shi'ite, 130
Sigismund, King of Hungary,
    47–48, 100, 167

Sixtus IV, Pope, 121
Skanderbeg, 56–58, 60–62,
    77–78, 86, 89, 101–2, 108–
    12
slavery, 3, 10, 15–17, 26, 29–
    30, 37–40, 44–45, 71–72,
    77, 85, 108, 111, 114, 118,
    120, 128, 132, 135–136,
    142–48, 150–51, 153–54,
    159–60, 164, 168, 171–72,
    174, 189, 194, 200–1, 216,
    221
Smederevo, 89, 94–95
Sobieski, Jan, King of Poland,
    206–7
Society of Jesus, 148, 182, 191,
    199
Sokollu, Mehmed, 185, 187–88,
    195–96
Speyer, Diet of, 166, 171
Starhemberg, Count, 204
Suleiman I, (the Magnificent),
    131–33, 135, 137–42, 146,
    148, 152–53, 155, 157, 163–
    65, 170–73, 175, 178, 180,
    185–87
Suleiman II, Sultan, 209
Suleyman, (Bey), Pasha, 25, 28
Sunni, 63, 217
Sura, 5, 14–15, *see also Qur'an*
Szigetvár, 175, 178–80

Tamerlane, 51–52, 216
Te Deum, 173, 207
Thirty Years' War, 182, 196–98
Thököly, Imre, 201
Thomas, St. Peter, 32–33

Tomas (Tomasovic), Stefan, King
    of Bosnia, 95–99, 104
Tomori, Archbishop of Kalocsa,
    167–69
Tours/Poitiers, Battle of, 12
Transylvania, 56, 181–82, 210–
    11
Trent, Council of, 182

uniate, 66, 72
Union of Florence, 54–55, 64–
    65, 85, 96, 135
Urban II, Pope Bl., 33, 90
Urban IV, Pope, 20
Urban V, Pope Bl., 34, 36
Uzun-Hasan, 102, 111, 114

Varna, Crusade of, 55, 57, 60,
    78, 92, 95
Vincent de Paul, St., 144–45
Vlad II Dracul, King of Wal-
    lachia, 100
Vlad III, the Impaler, King of
    Wallachia, 100–1
Vladislav V, King of Hungary
    and Poland, 55, 60
Vukcic, Stefan, 97–99

Wallachia, 100–2
Wolsey, Cardinal, 131
World War I, 211, 222

Ye'or, Bat, 16, 18, 74, 224, 226

Zapolya, János, 171, 173, 178
Zenta, Battle of, 211
Zrinyi, Miklos, 179–80